"*This wonderfully crafted, deeply researched narrative takes us to different places in Washington, D.C., where Filipino and American lives came together. Tiongson guides us through streets and alleys, from the National Mall to the Union Street train station. He leads us through spaces in the District of Columbia, relating tales of interchange, often in serendipitous ways. Filipino leaders for example made pilgrimages to the U.S. capital, making their varied cases for Philippine independence. Lives were touched, ideas flowed, and spaces transformed, both in the U.S. and the Philippines. Tiongson delightfully reminds us of the significance of place in the saga of the intertwined lives of both nations and their peoples.*"

—*Felice Noelle Rodriguez, Philippine historian and Visiting Professor, Ateneo de Zamboanga University*

———

"*This book is an essential guide for those interested in seeing Washington, D.C., and its sites from a Philippine perspective, i.e., from the vantage point of a former American colony on the circuitous road to independence. Through storytelling and rare historical gems, Professor Tiongson fills in gaps in the Filipino-American narrative, reminding us that we were at once subjects of the American Empire as well as friends. Philippine-American Heritage in Washington, D.C. is more like a juicy 'Insider's Guide' to a vexed Fil-Am history than a city guide book. Coming at a time when the Philippines and the United States might need to unite against military aggression in the Pacific anew, this book links us back to our shared wartime history and an extraordinary generation of leaders. This is a newly relevant, important read for Filipinos and Americans alike.*"

—*Liana Romulo, author and Archivist of the Carlos P. Romulo Foundation for Peace and Development*

PHILIPPINE-AMERICAN HERITAGE
IN
Washington, D.C.

ERWIN R. TIONGSON

THE
History
PRESS

Published by The History Press
Charleston, SC
www.historypress.com

First published 2023

Manufactured in the United States

ISBN 9781467149020

Library of Congress Control Number: 2022948304

Notice: The information in this book is true and complete to the best of our knowledge. It is offered without guarantee on the part of the author or The History Press. The author and The History Press disclaim all liability in connection with the use of this book.

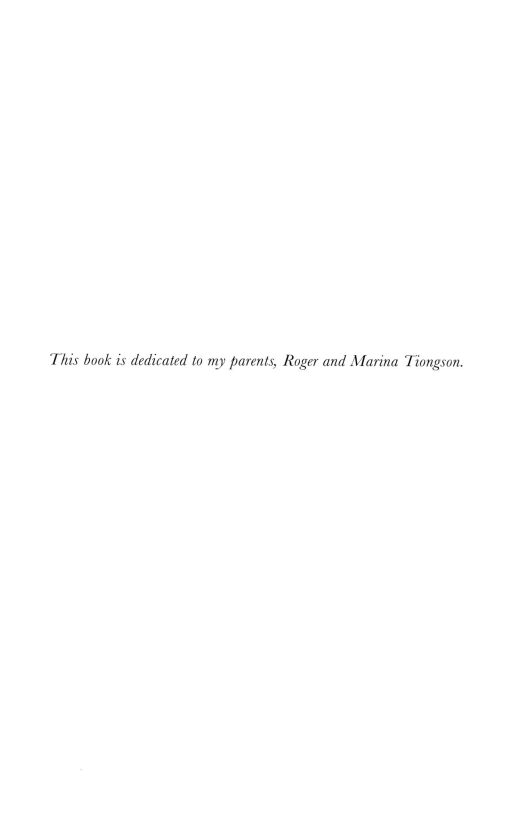

This book is dedicated to my parents, Roger and Marina Tiongson.

Contents

Acknowledgements

*T*his book grew out of a family research project, the Philippines on the Potomac (POPDC) Project, that I co-founded in 2012 and have co-managed with Teresa Carandang together with our children, Nicolas and Rafael Tiongson. All the relevant POPDC publications are cited in the bibliography. I am thankful for the support and encouragement of numerous colleagues and friends over the years, including (in alphabetical order) Rita Cacas, Laura Caron, JV Chan-Gonzaga, Malcolm and Nita Churchill, Hank Hendrickson, Noelle Rodriguez, Liana Romulo and Nila Toribio-Straka. I am always grateful to my brother Hector and my sister-in-law Woweene Ledesma for their care. I would also like to thank Ricky Lim, Binggay Montilla and Manolo Quezon for generously sharing photographs from their family's collection and Hector for helping me take many of the photographs featured in this volume. I appreciate Ryan Finn's expert and tireless editorial support, from which the book has greatly benefited. I am particularly grateful to my acquisitions editor at The History Press, Kate Jenkins, whose expertise, kindness and patience made it possible for me to complete this manuscript during an extraordinary period.

Introduction

Halfway across the world, the Philippines would seem far removed from daily life in Washington, D.C., and its surrounding areas. But the two are deeply intertwined, with a bond that is strong yet little known and insufficiently documented. In 1898, following the end of the Spanish-American War, the Philippines was annexed by the United States and remained a U.S. colony until the United States recognized its independence in 1946. This period, spanning nearly half a century, frames many stories of the Philippine presence in Washington. But this presence runs deeper and longer than the colonial period, and the histories, politics and humanity of the Philippines still abound throughout time and place in D.C.

This introduction provides a brief overview of Philippine-American history, highlighting key figures and their ties to the capital and, in some cases, to very specific D.C. neighborhoods. This chapter also provides a framework to help understand how the nature of this Philippine-American presence has evolved over time, mirroring the evolution of Philippine-American relations more broadly and representing milestones in nation-building, the preparation for independence from the United States and the years after.

In the late 1890s, Philippine-American ties were personified by leading figures in the Spanish-American War, such as Admiral George Dewey, who had defeated the Spanish armada at the Battle of Manila Bay in May 1898, and President William McKinley himself, along with his senior cabinet officials, such as those who negotiated the terms of the annexation of the

Philippines, despite General Emilio Aguinaldo's declaration of Philippine independence in June 1898. In succeeding years, as the twentieth century dawned, Philippine-American ties to Washington would evolve to include American military officials like General John Pershing and General Peyton March, both of whom had served in the brutal Philippine-American War, and eventually American civilian officials like President William Howard Taft, who previously served as the first U.S. civilian governor general in the Philippines, as the conflict ceased and the U.S. transitioned to institution-building in its newly acquired territory. This period would also bring into Washington Philippine officials of the new colonial administration, including the succession of resident commissioners, who were nonvoting members of U.S. Congress—future Philippine Commonwealth president Manuel L. Quezon being one of them—and young Filipino scholars, the *pensionados*, who were sent to the U.S. for graduate studies in preparation for public service. A good number of these young professionals were educated at George Washington University (GWU) and Georgetown University and later took on leading roles in Philippine government, including as chief justice of the Philippine Supreme Court.

Following the passage of the Jones Act in 1916, named after Virginia congressman William Atkinson Jones, the United States formally promised recognition of Philippine independence, created a freely elected bicameral Philippine legislature and granted Filipinos more positions in government and "as large a control of domestic affairs as can be given them," as the act reads. American officials like Francis Burton Harrison, who was once a member of U.S. Congress and a Washington resident and later served as governor general of the Philippines, moved quickly to implement the new law to allow more Filipinos to assume responsibility for government affairs. Upon arrival in Manila at the start of his term, Harrison announced that "every step we take will be with a view to the ultimate independence of the islands and as a preparation for that independence." The United States, he once declared, "had no justification for holding those people in bondage."

But actual independence would take another thirty years. Through the 1920s and the 1930s, the Philippines sent numerous independence missions to Washington to lobby for independence. The leaders of these missions were often important figures in Philippine-American history, including those who later became Philippine presidents, such as Quezon, Sergio Osmeña and Manuel Roxas. In parallel, civic leaders like Sofia de Veyra served as their country's cultural ambassadors, educating Americans about Philippine life and its readiness for independence.

Meanwhile, this colonial relationship made it possible for Filipinos to move to the United States, work for the government or in the private sector, form families and build new lives in the metro D.C. area. Many of these first migrants, for example, were mess men in the U.S. Navy, government clerks or Washington cab drivers. Their work and the lives they built in the region are featured in a volume written by Rita Cacas and Juanita Tamayo Lott, *Filipinos in Washington, D.C.*, published in 2009.

In 1934, the U.S. Congress passed the Philippine Independence Act, which created the Philippine Commonwealth and initiated a ten-year transition to U.S. recognition of Philippine independence. But this, too, was delayed as the Second World War broke out. Enemies at the beginning of the twentieth century, Filipino and American soldiers now found themselves fighting side by side against Japanese soldiers. In 1942, Japan occupied the Philippines, forcing the Philippine Commonwealth government into exile in Washington. President Quezon and his family

Philippine Commonwealth president Manuel Quezon and U.S. President Franklin D. Roosevelt at Union Station, May 1942. *From left to right*: First Lady Aurora Quezon, Manuel Quezon Jr., President Manuel Quezon, President Franklin Roosevelt, Captain John McCrea, Maria Aurora Quezon, Zeneida Quezon and Vice President Sergio Osmena. *Franklin D. Roosevelt Presidential Library and Museum.*

stayed in a suite at the Shoreham Hotel north of Dupont Circle. They also stayed briefly at the Belmont Country Club (then known simply as Belmont or the Patrick Hurley estate) in Ashburn, Virginia.

General Douglas MacArthur led Philippine and American forces in Leyte in late 1944, beginning the long, violent campaign to liberate the Philippines. The Japanese occupation ended in 1945, and the Philippines finally became an independent republic the following year, ushering in a new period in U.S.-Philippine relations. The notable events marking this new relationship include state visits of postwar Philippine presidents, their stay at the Blair House and, in one rare case, an address before a joint session of U.S. Congress at the Capitol. There have also been new streams of Philippine students and scholars, artists and writers and cohorts of immigrants finding new homes in Washington. The year 2021 marked the seventy-fifth year of formal diplomatic ties between the United States and the Philippines as a sovereign nation, commemorated in a program of activities organized by the Philippine embassy together with U.S. State Department representatives.

A closer look into two prominent Filipino lives in the twentieth century captures the forces at work during this time. Both are extraordinary in their achievements, and their presence mirrors the evolving Philippine ties to Washington. As a consequence, they are a recurring presence across distinct periods in Philippine-American history and across neighborhoods of Washington and chapters of this book.

One is Quezon, who had first visited the United States in 1908, received an audience with President Theodore Roosevelt and was surprised by the president's "simplicity and democratic manners." Quezon was familiar with European formalities, and he "never suspected that America had truly discarded their ways and ceremonial practices," as he wrote in his memoirs. In December 1909, he first moved to Washington as a resident commissioner and found a temporary home on K Street. ("So I spent my first Christmas Eve in Washington duly shut up in my rooms in the Champlain Apartment House," he wrote in his memoirs.) Although he left Washington in 1916 shortly after his new friends in the U.S. Congress passed the Jones Act, his role as Philippine Senate president over the following decade and a half brought him frequently back to the city as he led various missions to lobby for independence. After securing the Philippine Independence Act of 1934, he became president of the Philippine Commonwealth. He appeared again frequently in Washington, but this time as the leader of a nearly independent country. As the Second World War sent his government into exile in 1942, he returned to Washington once more, living there along with his family and

Bataan Street. The Philippine embassy is in the background. *Photo by the author.*

the members of his cabinet. He died on August 1, 1944, still in exile, and was temporarily buried in Arlington, never seeing his country's complete independence.

The other is Carlos P. Romulo—Pulitzer Prize winner, World War II general, president of the United Nations (UN) General Assembly and the Philippines' most senior diplomat in the postwar period. His ties to Washington reflect a remarkable, ascendant career and milestones of Philippine-American history as well as world history. He first visited

Washington around 1921 as a government scholar studying in New York. He had thought of Taft as a "father image" ("Benign, paternal and kindly, he kept an eye on my reports and always interested in knowing how I was getting along," Romulo wrote) and was Taft's "frequent house guest." In Washington and New York, he saw firsthand America's promise ("This is life," he thought, "in a nation that had reached its full development"), as well as its prejudice, particularly the harsh treatment of African Americans ("a depressed people huddled together in freedom's land"), something he himself had experienced in the Philippines. Romulo recalled his shock at first seeing Washington's slums. ("I could not understand why a country as rich as America would permit such conditions to exist," he wrote in his memoirs.) About a year later, he came back to Washington as a member of an independence mission, advocating for his own country's freedom. In the late 1920s, as a young journalist and as an administrator and lecturer at the University of the Philippines (UP), he visited Washington again as the coach of the UP debate team in competition with the GWU team, on the question of granting the Philippines independence. He served on other independence missions, and in the 1940s, he was an official of the Commonwealth Government-in-Exile. He survived the war and became a national symbol as he marked its end in a ceremony in front of the Old Philippine Chancery on Massachusetts Avenue. In the postwar period, he became the principal representative of a newly independent country and a resident of Garfield Street. He was also a global leader and a signatory of the United Nations Charter, and he served as president of the Fourth UN General Assembly. In 1961, largely through his efforts, two streets near the Philippine Chancery were named "Bataan" and "Corregidor," after the sites of two of the most important Philippine battles of the Second World War. At the ceremony naming them, he spoke of "the close ties of friendship which bind the peoples of the United States and the Philippines"—ties that influenced and were in turn influenced by his work and life.

These two consequential figures in history have helped shape the lives of countless people, the interwoven destinies of the United States and the Philippines and, at least in Romulo's case, the landscape of their adopted city. It is this city's neighborhoods and their Philippine-American ties that we now explore in the following chapters.

The National Mall
and Capitol Hill

National Mall

"The National Mall—the great swath of green in the middle of our capital city and stretching from the foot of the United States Capitol to the Potomac River," according to the National Park Service (NPS), "is the premier civic and symbolic space in our nation." But this space, so central to Washington, D.C., was not the only of its kind. The National Mall also inspired a central feature of a 1905 plan for Manila designed by the celebrated Chicago architect Daniel Burnham.

Burnham visited in the Philippines in December 1904. He had been sent to the Philippines at the recommendation of Philippine commissioner W. Cameron Forbes and William Howard Taft, who had served as governor general of the Philippines and was then secretary of war. His task was to help produce, as Burnham wrote, "a plan for connecting thoroughfares, open spaces, driveways and promenades which should provide adequate facilities for transportation, improved sanitation, and opportunities for those particular kinds of recreation which the climate invites."

Taft himself recalled Burnham's trip, writing, "Without pay, at my instance, he visited the Philippine Islands in order to make plans for the beautification of Manila and for the laying out of a capital in the mountains in the fine climate of Baguio." Burnham spent about six weeks "talking with government officials, inspecting and surveying the pertinent sites, working over maps and 'on the ground,' and enjoying,

Aerial view of the National Mall, Washington, D.C. *Carol M. Highsmith Archive, Library of Congress, Prints and Photographs Division.*

besides, considerable socializing and sight-seeing," according to historian Thomas Hines.

In June 1905, Burnham, together with his associate Peirce Anderson, submitted their "plan of proposed improvements"—two maps accompanied by a report. The plan proposed, among other key features, the development of waterfronts, parks and waterways; an enhanced street system; and specific sites for buildings and other activities. "It had a central civic core; radials emanating from this core were laid over a gridiron pattern and large parks interconnected by parkways," according to Philippine architect and historian Paulo Alcazaren. "In the central civic core, which he located beside the old city, the government buildings were arranged in a formal pattern around a rectangular mall." The plan also envisaged a larger Luneta Park, Manila's central park, "with the Government Plaza east of it."

The similarities between D.C. and the National Mall were unmistakable and unsurprising, as Burnham himself led the commission that prepared the redesign of the National Mall just a few years earlier. "Resembling Washington D.C. in both appearance and plan," according to historian Ian Morley, "Filipinos' capacity to see the new governmental core was to encourage them to look with esteem towards the symbol of the American presence in the Philippine archipelago: the dome of the Capitol." Some observers also imagine a striking resemblance between the Washington Monument and the Rizal Monument, both of which feature an obelisk, although this particular detail was not in Burnham's plan for Manila and was likely due more to the shared masonic affiliation of Washington and José Rizal, the Philippine National Hero.

WEST POTOMAC PARK

Such inspiration in architecture and public spaces flowed both ways. Manila, too, boasted an important and influential park at its core. "The Luneta's conceptual similarity to the national mall in Washington, D.C. can hardly be missed," historian Daniel Doeppers wrote, referring to Manila's large historic park near Intramuros, "but the centuries-old city wall gives it an even greater time depth." And, remarkably, Manila's Luneta Park itself would subsequently reshape Washington's landscape.

Both William Howard Taft and his wife, Helen Herron Taft, had lived in the Philippines while Taft was governor general, and they had spent many evenings listening to the Philippine Constabulary Band (see the next chapter) perform at the Luneta. The space impressed her greatly. "That Manila could lend anything to Washington may be a surprise to some persons," the first lady wrote, "but the Luneta is an institution whose usefulness to society in the Philippine capital is not to be overestimated." When William became U.S. president in 1909, Helen immediately began working, as she wrote in her memoirs, to "convert Potomac Park into a glorified Luneta, where all Washington could meet, either on foot, or in vehicles, at five o'clock on certain evenings, listen to band concerts and enjoy such recreation as no other spot in Washington could afford."

On Saturday afternoon, April 17, 1909, just a little over a month after President Taft's inauguration, Helen led the inauguration of West Potomac Park. She launched a new concert series on park grounds, featuring the Philippine Constabulary Band itself, which had also performed at Taft's inauguration. Among those in attendance were Admiral George Dewey and his wife (see "Downtown Washington" chapter), Alice Roosevelt Longworth (see "Dupont Circle and Neighborhood" chapter) and several thousand others. "Everybody saw everybody that he or she knew," Helen wrote, "and there was the same exchange of friendly greetings that had always made the Luneta such a pleasant meeting place." The series was immediately hailed as "already assuming a place in Washington life similar to that played by Hyde

Vintage postcard of West Potomac Park Bandstand and Speedway, 1910. *Author's collection.*

Park in London or the Bois de Bologne in Paris," changing the city's social life. "Potomac Park became the city's most fashionable afternoon spot from April to late October," architectural historian Nenette Arroyo wrote in the *White House History Quarterly*.

Newspapers celebrated the Taft administration's "complete social success," which was thanks to Helen's pioneering efforts, according to her biographer, Lewis Gould. She had electrified the city by ignoring many social conventions for a woman of the period: she smoked, she drove an automobile on her own along D.C.'s new Speedway (which she renamed Potomac Drive) and she was an avid poker player. She had, according to the National First Ladies' Library, a "self-proclaimed taste for quality beer and champagne." At William's inauguration, she insisted on riding next to her husband—a first. "Mrs. Taft is to smash all precedents on inauguration day," the *New York Times* announced ahead of the inauguration. "Perhaps," she wrote in her memoirs, "I had a little secret elation in thinking that I was doing something which no woman had done before."

Helen even put together one of D.C.'s most notable botanic attractions. Sometime after the inauguration of West Potomac Park, she received a letter from Eliza Scidmore, a travel writer who worked for *National Geographic* and the *New York Times*. Scidmore's mother had previously met Helen Taft in

President and Mrs. Taft in White House automobile, 1909. *Library of Congress, Prints and Photographs Division.*

Japan, and Scidmore suggested planting Japanese cherry blossoms in the city. The mayor of Tokyo heard about these plans through a Japanese consul and donated two thousand young trees. Although the first batch of trees arrived disease-ridden, the mayor sent thousands more as replacement. Since these trees were planted, countless tourists have visited D.C. each springtime to see the pink and white cherry blossoms along the Tidal Basin, East Potomac Park and West Potomac Park, unaware of their Philippine origins.

The two cities, D.C. and Manila, evolved together. At the request of U.S. colonial administrators in the Philippines, Burnham produced a plan for Manila based on D.C., with Luneta as a central element of this plan. But with help from Helen Taft, these colonial ties have been mutually transformative, as Luneta itself reshaped D.C., its geography and its social life, with springtime souvenirs that have lasted for more than a century.

CAPITOL BUILDING

In September 1986, a large crowd gathered on Capitol Hill for a rare standing room–only joint session of U.S. Congress. The occasion was an address by Philippine president Corazon Aquino, just months after the

People Power Revolution that ended the Marcos dictatorship and made her president. She was a "housewife" but found herself thrust into public life when her husband, Senator Benigno (Ninoy) Aquino, was assassinated three years earlier. Many in the audience wore her trademark color—yellow blouses and shirts—and they had scattered yellow roses along her path. Her speech was interrupted numerous times by lively applause, "led by Filipino-Americans cheering from the galleries," the *Washington Post* wrote.

She had come to Washington, D.C., to request aid for her country as her administration began the rehabilitation of an impoverished economy. "You have spent many lives and much treasure to bring freedom to many lands that were reluctant to receive it," she told her audience. "And here you have a people who won it by themselves and need only help to preserve it." She received an enthusiastic response. The House immediately "bypassed normal procedures to approve a $200 million emergency aid package for the Philippines," the *Washington Post* noted.

There is a sense that this moment in Aquino's presidency was made possible decades prior by her predecessor, Manuel L. Quezon, and his remarkable political career. Quezon had won the promise of independence, and women won the right to vote during his commonwealth presidency. His career, too, reached a milestone in the same Capitol building in 1910, as he served as his country's resident commissioner. "My service in the House of Representatives was one of the most pleasant and fruitful periods of my life," Quezon wrote in his memoirs. "No one can possibly imagine how much of human value there is to be found under the two wings of the Capitol."

Quezon's national political career is, in fact, framed by addresses before members of U.S. Congress. In May 1910, just months after his arrival in Washington, in a language he had just learned to speak, he spoke movingly of the "benefits which we had received from the Government of the United States." "But despite it all," he told his audience, "we still want independence." Thirty-two years later, in June 1942, as the commonwealth president in exile on the eve of promised independence, he addressed the House and the Senate again, on two separate occasions. "Speaker Rayburn welcomed him as the chief executive of a valorous people," the *Evening Star* wrote, "and as former member of the House itself." In the shadow of the fall of Bataan and Corregidor, Quezon vowed that the Philippine people would continue to fight together with the United States until their enemies were defeated and his country's freedom was won. He was "loudly applauded," the *Evening Star* wrote. Quezon died in 1944, months before the liberation of the Philippines and two years before its complete independence.

In September 1986, Aquino stood inside this building in the shadow of her own incalculable loss. "Three years ago I left America in grief, to bury my husband, Ninoy Aquino," she told members of U.S. Congress. "I thought I had left it also, to lay to rest his restless dream of Philippine freedom. Today, I have returned as the President of a free people."

THE NATIONAL GALLERY OF ART

The National Gallery of Art, which began as a gift of 152 artworks from industrialist Andrew Mellon, currently has some 150,000 works of art in its collection, which, as this national museum states, "spans the history of Western art and showcases some of the triumphs of human creativity." Among these great works of art, the museum shares many ties with the Filipino American community, stretching from the art in its collections to the workers who have kept the museum safe and running throughout its tenure.

Among the museum's vast collection are the abstract expressionist works of Filipino American artist Alfonso Ossorio, including etchings, watercolors and wood engravings. Ossorio was one of the six children of Miguel Ossorio, founder of a sugar milling company called the Victorias Milling Company, in the central part of the Philippines. The Catholic chapel at Victorias features a large, remarkable mural by Ossorio known as the *Angry Christ*, and hence the Church of St. Joseph the Worker is more widely known as the "Church of the Angry Christ."

Ossorio himself was a patron of fellow abstract expressionists in the United States, in particular Jackson Pollock and Jean Dubuffet. He owned some of their works, which now belong to the permanent collection of the museum. One of them, Pollock's *Number 1, 1950 (Lavender Mist)*, is currently on display in the East Building. Their correspondence from this period reflects this dimension of their relationship. "Dear Jackson," a 1951 letter from Ossorio to Pollock preserved by the Smithsonian begins, "In my last letter to Lee I enclosed $200 to be applied towards the next painting of yours we acquire."

The National Gallery of Art is also home to the papers and personal histories of the Monuments, Fine Arts and Archives (MFAA), otherwise known as the Monuments Men. Made popular by a 2014 Hollywood film starring Cate Blanchett and George Clooney, the MFAA is a group of about 345 men and women who worked with the Allied Forces beginning around 1945, at the end of the Second World War, to help recover artworks and personal possessions stolen by the Nazis and restore them to their owners.

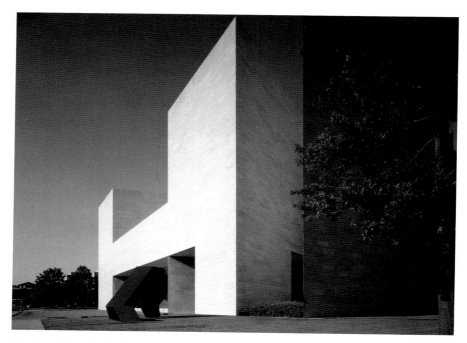

The East Wing of the National Gallery of Art, Washington, D.C. *Carol M. Highsmith Archive, Library of Congress, Prints and Photographs Division.*

Among the Monuments Men was Ossorio's younger brother, Frederic, who had studied art history at Yale University prior to the war and in his work with the MFAA helped recover a Van Gogh concealed in a salt mine.

The museum's Philippine ties also go deeper into its workings, featuring at least one member of the pioneer migrant Philippine community in the metro D.C. area—whose lives are documented in the book by Rita Cacas and Juanita Tamayo Lott, *Filipinos in Washington, D.C.* U.S. Army veteran Moises Bautista was a member of the museum's security force beginning in the late 1940s, just a few years after the establishment of the museum, until his retirement in 1975. (Outside his work hours at the museum, Bautista drove a cab, like other members of the Filipino American community during that period, to help make ends meet.) Bautista's name is on the roster of employees in several volumes of the gallery's annual report, and he appears alongside other museum guards in a 1971 group photograph featured in Cacas and Lott's book, taken in front of the West Building.

Bautista's tenure coincided with the wealthy Mellon's son Paul, who had a long association with the gallery—as a trustee after the war, then as vice-president and eventually as president. In his memoirs, *Reflections in a Silver Spoon*, Paul Mellon gives a sense of what the National Gallery of Art must have been like in its early years, as he recalled walking around a near-empty building. "Personally I found the paucity of paintings in relationship to the available wall space mildly depressing," he wrote, "and this feeling was echoed in a sly joke at the time pointing out that the guards were there not so much to protect the works of art as to guide visitors to the next painting." Bautista was assigned to one of the gallery's two entrances and remembered seeing Paul Mellon often, according to an unpublished account that he shared with Cacas. Mellon was a "really nice gentleman" and treated him with "great kindness and respect," Bautista said.

THE LIBRARY OF CONGRESS

The Library of Congress is said to be the biggest library worldwide and counts millions of books, manuscripts, photographs, recordings and other archival materials in its enormous collection. Among its numerous treasures—including the Declaration of Independence, the Emancipation Proclamation and the Gutenberg Bible—is one of the first books printed in the Philippines, the *Doctrina Christiana, en lengua española y tagala*, printed in 1593 and now in the Lessing J. Rosenwald Collection of the library. Philippine historian Carlos Quirino lists three known *Doctrinas* from the late 1500s: this *Doctrina*, a Chinese *Doctrina* in the Vatican library and another Chinese *Doctrina* in Madrid's Biblioteca Nacional (which Quirino calls the "Tratado" and is known as "Shih-lu" in other scholarly writings).

Printed in both the Roman alphabet and the pre-Spanish alphabet in the Philippines, this *Doctrina* features Catholic catechism and well-known prayers, such as the Lord's Prayer. Edwin Wolf II, an American librarian who wrote the introduction to the reprint of the *Doctrina*, credits several priests as the authors of the work.

How the book has been preserved for more than four hundred years is a source of bibliographic wonder and mystery. The book is printed on mulberry, "one of the most destructible papers ever used in book production," Wolf wrote. "The native worms and insects thrived on it, and the heat and dampness took their slower but equally certain toll. Add to these enemies the acts of providence of which the Philippines have received more than their share—earthquake, fire and flood—and the man-made devastations of war." But somehow the book survived. "One copy of this Doctrina was sent

The domes of the Library of Congress Thomas Jefferson Building and the U.S. Capitol, Washington, D.C. *Carol M. Highsmith Archive, Library of Congress, Prints and Photographs Division.*

to Philip II by the Governor of the Philippines in 1593," Wolf said, "and in 1785 a Jesuit philologist, Hervas y Panduro, printed Tagalog texts from a then extant copy." Not much is known about the book after 1785, until its discovery in 1946.

The broad storyline of its twentieth-century discovery is well known and recounted in several articles, including Wolf's own piece. In early 1946, William Schab, a New York bookseller, found the book in Paris. From there, a book collector and philanthropist named Lessing Rosenwald purchased the book from Schab and immediately donated it to the Library of Congress. "Where the book had been before it reached Paris we do not know," Wolf said. Quirino later traced the book's story a few years earlier, to around late 1942, when Luigi Banzi, a Bologna bookseller, acquired it "from a school teacher of the Romagna region." Quirino claims that the book "belonged to a peasant family whose forebears had lived or visited the Philippines late in the sixteenth century." It was then sold to a "Paris collector," from whom Schab purchased the book in 1946, Quirino said.

To this provenance, we can add one more layer of prior ownership, the possible identity of this "Paris collector." A clue comes from the recollections of Schab's colleague, H.P. Kraus, who called this the "Galanti Caper," after Blasio Galanti. Galanti was "the most mysterious bookseller in Paris," Kraus wrote, and every trip to Paris required a "pilgrimage to Galanti." Galanti owned "the finest stocks of choice books and manuscripts in Paris" but "preferred not to display them to browsers." He kept his most prized possessions in his bedroom, away from most customers. In the main office, "stacks of miscellaneous books ringed the floor," making it nearly impossible to browse. Patience Gray, an English writer, recalled meeting Galanti and described him as "a wonderful emaciated figure, whose sad face reminded me of Italy's early 19th century revolutionaries." Gray remembers the same gigantic stacks of books. Galanti's house, Gray said, "had practically disappeared beneath static piles of books."

"Atop one book mountain," Kraus recalled, he and Schab "discovered a blockbook printed in strange eastern and Latin characters. The title-page imprint read Manila, 1593." Having read a book on Philippine bibliography, Kraus recalled a reference to a "ghost book"—"a Doctrina Cristiana…in Spanish and Tagalog"—but "no actual specimen had been seen." They bought the book for "a very modest price," Kraus recalled. Galanti, despite his vast bibliographic knowledge, must have been less familiar with early Philippine printing. "I knew I had a treasure in my hands," Kraus said.

Today, this treasure endures at the Library of Congress. The book bears witness both to the richness of early Philippine culture and to its own journey—and the journey of Philippine language and history—around the world.

THE U.S. HOLOCAUST MEMORIAL MUSEUM

The Holocaust Museum is dedicated to preserving Holocaust history, remembering its victims and survivors and inspiring people to "confront hatred, prevent genocide, and promote human dignity." Located next to the National Mall, its permanent exhibit features artifacts, audio and video footage and heart-wrenching personal testimonials on the terrible history of the Holocaust. Among the museum's collections are archival items, photographs and videos documenting the lives of members of the Jewish community in Manila. About 1,200 Jewish refugees arrived in the Philippines in the late 1930s after escaping Nazi Germany and finding an adopted home in the Philippines.

One of these refugees was Frank Ephraim, who was a D.C. resident and a graduate of George Washington University and who was in his later years a docent of the museum. He was among the first in recent years to write about his experience. His book, *Escape to Manila*, was published in 2003, a few years before he passed away, and contains vivid accounts of lighter moments in his family's life in Manila just before the war. ("One of the joys on Dewey Boulevard were the Magnolia ice cream vendors," he wrote about the main road along Manila Bay's shoreline, and the most affordable item was a "chocolate flavored popsicle.") He also wrote about the horrors of the Japanese occupation. He described a Jewish man caught giving cigarettes to a prisoner. "They had hung him upside down and had jammed lighted matches under his fingernails," Ephraim wrote, "to make him confess to 'aiding the enemy.'" When Manuel L. Quezon died while in exile overseas, Ephraim recalled, the Jewish community in the Philippines grieved. "Who could forget his determined speech welcoming the immigration of Jewish refugees at the dedication of the Jewish home in Marikina in 1940, on land he had provided?" Ephraim wrote.

Among the many stories in Ephraim's book is a moving account of a postwar musical performance led by Herbert Zipper, the Austrian-born conductor, composer and Dachau survivor who served as conductor of the prewar Manila Symphony Orchestra (MSO). (Zipper had first arrived in Manila in June 1939. "I was there at the pier with my parents that day and witnessed the scene," Ephraim wrote.) In 1945, as the Second World War drew to a close, Zipper gathered the surviving members of the orchestra and all the musical instruments they could find, determined to perform a concert to celebrate the liberation of Europe and Manila, Zipper's temporary home.

Few thought that Zipper would succeed in the wake of the devastation left by the Japanese occupation. Several MSO musicians had died during the occupation or left the city. The head of the woodwinds section had been killed, according to Zipper's biography, and the concert master had been "burned to death with his townspeople," according to Ephraim. The musicians who did survive seemed "too weak from malnutrition to play," according to one account, including Zipper himself, who looked "emaciated over three years of privation." And no one had played in an orchestra for years.

But Zipper was determined. He started rehearsals in April, collected instruments "miraculously salvaged from the fires" and went around Manila gathering chairs for the audience. For weeks, Zipper could be seen "tirelessly driving, begging, coaching, teaching." Finally, one evening in May, in the midst of the remains of Santa Cruz Cathedral and with about 2,400 people in attendance, Zipper and his orchestra played Beethoven's *Eroica* and Dvořák's *New World Symphony*. Historian Benito Legarda Jr., who sat on the front row, recalled that the program began at 7:20 p.m. and soon "the concert proper was underway, with the first thundering chords of the mighty Eroica signaling the start of a new era for the country." War correspondent William J. Dunn wrote a moving account of the evening. "What remained of this orchestra performed the Eroica from a makeshift stage in the nave of Santa Cruz, what was left of one of Manila's most ancient churches, the music echoing between the shattered walls and soaring to the tropical sky that provided the only roof," Dunn said. "It was at once a paean of joy and a prayer of thanksgiving."

A half century later, in October 1995, a program was held at the museum in honor of Zipper. The occasion also marked the launch of a book and a documentary about Zipper's remarkable life. Ephraim was a volunteer that evening, and they spoke. Zipper, who was then ninety-one years old, was "bent with age, but still as dynamic a personality as ever," Ephraim recalled.

UNION STATION AND NEIGHBORHOOD

UNION STATION

Just steps away from the Capitol and the National Mall, Union Station serves as a train station and a multimodal transportation hub—one can catch a bus, rent a car or ride a subway to various points in the metro D.C. area—and as a shopping center. The station was designed by Chicago architect Daniel Burnham, who also prepared the plans for Manila (see the previous chapter) and Baguio, a city on a Philippine mountaintop, at the beginning of the U.S. colonial period in the Philippines.

It is also a special place in Philippine-American history, the site of milestones in the transformation of two nations. With D.C. some distance away from the coasts, most of the first Philippine visitors and migrants during the first half of the twentieth century would have arrived by train, and Union Station would have been their arrival point. In fact, there are records of official Philippine delegations being received by American and Filipino officials right here. ("Arriving at the Union Station at 8 a.m., the [Philippine independence] commissioners were greeted by Pedro Guevara, senior resident commissioner and Mrs. Roxas, who came to Washington from a European tour recently to await her husband's arrival," the *Evening Star* wrote in January 1930.) Two of these arrivals are noteworthy.

In 1933, members of the Visayan Circle—a Filipino community association in Washington that organized social events and also purchased the property that eventually became the Manila House (see "Foggy

Above: Philippine Commonwealth president Manuel Quezon and U.S. President Franklin D. Roosevelt at Union Station, May 1942. *Courtesy of the Quezon Family Collection.*

Right: Quezon and Roosevelt at Union Station, May 1942. *Franklin D. Roosevelt Presidential Library & Museum.*

Bottom" chapter)—gathered at Union Station to welcome the Philippine Independence Delegation, led by Manuel L. Quezon and accompanied by fellow future president Elpidio Quirino and other Philippine officials. Just like the other missions dating back to 1919, they were here to lobby the U.S. government for Philippine independence. Earlier, a mission led by Sergio Osmeña and Manuel Roxas, also known as the Os-Rox mission, successfully secured an independence bill—the Hare, Hawes, Cutting Act—which was ultimately rejected by the Philippine Senate. Quezon's mission secured another independence act, the Tydings-McDuffie Law (also known as the 1934 Philippine Independence Act). This time, the act was endorsed by the Philippine Senate and led to the creation of the Philippine Commonwealth

Souvenir panoramic photography of members of the Visayan Circle meeting Manuel Quezon at Union Station, December 7, 1933. Florentine Calabia is fourth from left (*standing, arms folded*), and Nestora Calabia is second to Quezon's right. *Courtesy of the Rita M. Cacas Filipino American Community Archives in the University of Maryland Libraries Special Collections.*

Government and the ten-year preparation for independence. Quezon and Quirino were present at President Roosevelt's signing of the Tydings-McDuffie Law.

The locals who welcomed Quezon and his companions were among the first Philippine migrants in the metro D.C. area. Many of them arrived in the late 1920s and early 1930s. Some had moved from the West Coast in search of better prospects, some worked for the federal government, some drove taxicabs and some were in active duty or retired from the UN navy. Their journeys and the new lives they created in Washington have

been documented in the Cacas-Lott volume on Filipinos in Washington. Among them were Florentine and Nestora Calabia. Florentine had served with the U.S. Navy during the First World War, then traveled to the United States and later settled in the D.C. region in the early 1930s. Nestora was a schoolteacher in the Philippines who married Florentine, completed a law degree at Southeastern University and worked for years as an auditor in the U.S. General Accounting Office. ("Can you imagine the difficulty any woman would face in 1937—especially a woman lawyer who's an immigrant of color—to find a law job in D.C.?" her son Tino recalled at a public presentation in 2021.) She later served as president of the Filipino Women's Club in D.C. and organized social events and volunteer activities for its membership.

Quezon arrived at Union Station again in 1942, in a new national leadership role, and was met by a very different welcome committee. As the Second World War and the Japanese occupation of the Philippines sent him, his family and his colleagues in the Philippine government into exile, they traveled to Washington, D.C. This time, President Franklin D. Roosevelt himself was there to greet Quezon ("I found on our arrival in San Francisco that President Roosevelt had sent us a special railway train to bring us across the continent," Quezon wrote in his autobiography. "When we reached the Union Station in Washington, there stood the President himself to welcome us. Back of him I saw a reception committee made up of members of the Cabinet and of all the living Governors-General and High Commissioners of the past twenty years.") Quezon and his family stayed overnight at the White House (see "White House and Neighborhood" chapter).

National Postal Museum

Just steps away from the Union Station on Massachusetts Avenue is the Smithsonian's National Postal Museum, which, as the name suggests, features postal and philatelic history and artifacts. Among its collection are samples of Philippine stamps from distinct periods of Philippine history: the Spanish period, the U.S. administration from 1898 to 1935, the commonwealth period through 1946 and the period after independence. The museum also features temporary exhibits, which sometimes tie it even more closely to Philippine history.

A 2018 exhibit was called "My Fellow Soldiers: Letters from World War I," the title of which was drawn from a letter written in 1918 by General John Pershing, who led the American Expeditionary Force in Europe. Pershing had served in the Philippines until 1913, particularly in Mindanao, where he led the brutal Battle of Bud Bagsak in Jolo. Although the Philippine-American War officially ended in 1902, armed resistance would continue in parts of the Philippines, including the southern region of Mindanao, home of the country's Muslim communities. "The fighting was the fiercest I have ever seen," Pershing told his wife; his enemy combatants were "absolutely fearless." Two of Pershing's children were born while he was serving in the Philippines: Anne, in Baguio, and Mary Margaret, in Zamboanga. (His eldest daughter was born in Japan, and his son was born in the United States. "In the matter of birthplaces the family was a very mixed one," Pershing once said.)

The exhibit featured letters sent from Europe by soldiers, officers, nurses and civilians, including a 1915 letter from Pershing, whose wife and three daughters died in a house fire while Pershing was away. Only his son survived. "I am trying to work and keep from thinking but Oh! The desolation of life: the emptiness of it all, after such fullness as I have had," he told a friend. "I cannot think they are gone."

St. Aloysius Gonzaga Church and Gonzaga College High School

First constructed in 1859, St. Aloysius Gonzaga Church is a Roman Catholic church that served as a parish church until 2012 and is affiliated with a high school next door, a private preparatory school that bears the same name as the church, Gonzaga College High School. Both are run by the Jesuit priests, and they have at least two ties to Philippine-American history.

First, in June 1946, the *Evening Star* and the *Washington Post* announced that Miguel A. Bernad, the Filipino Jesuit and scholar, would lead his first mass at Gonzaga Church. In his long, distinguished academic career, Bernad published numerous books, including a volume on the lives of his fellow Philippine Jesuits (see "Georgetown" chapter). He visited Washington decades after, and an anthology of essays published in 1980 includes his gentle and erudite reflections on Washington life. Subway stations "are spacious and airy," he wrote, "vaulted tunnels as large as the baths of Caracalla." In the long escalator ride to the Dupont Circle station ("two and a half minutes"), he said, "I am always reminded of the line from Vergil, *facilis descensus Averno* (the descent is easy to the nether world)."

Joining in Bernad's celebration, according to the announcements, were four American Jesuits who had lived and worked in the Philippines in the prewar period. They included Nicholas Kunkel, SJ, a Baltimore native who was one of the founding teachers of a Jesuit high school in the Philippines, served briefly at Georgetown University as Prefect of Discipline and then returned to the Philippines to serve as dean of Ateneo de Manila University from the mid-1950s until the late 1960s (Kunkel was "sympathetic to new ideas and a great proponent of Filipinization," according to Philippine national artist Bienvenido Lumbera, who taught at the Ateneo for many years).

Second, the school's football field was once the home of Colonel Walter Loving, the African American conductor of the Philippine Constabulary

35

St. Aloysius Gonzaga Church, Washington, D.C. *Photo by the author.*

Band. It was a poor neighborhood through most of the twentieth century until its purchase and conversion in the 1970s. "Defrees Street, a one-block road that parallels H and I and dead ends at 1st and North Capitol, will be eliminated by the football field," the *Washington Post* reported in 1973.

Loving was born in Virginia, the child of former slaves. He was raised in Washington, D.C., by relatives in the 1890s and lived on 37 Defrees Street, according to historian and Loving's biographer, Robert Yoder. Loving attended the M Street School close to Gonzaga, the historic school for African Americans currently known as Dunbar High School, and was a member of its first class. He later served in the Philippines during the Philippine-American War.

Facing poor job prospects in D.C. in the early 1900s during a period of difficult race relations in the United States, Loving asked to be assigned to the Philippines again, just like other African Americans of his generation (in fact, some of them decided to live permanently in the Philippines upon their discharge or following the end of the Philippine-American War). "These men had no desire to return to America's racial animosity that, at its worst, included the continuing horror of lynching, as well as oppressive state laws requiring segregation and producing racial disfranchisement," according to military historian Roger Cunningham. In large part due to his outstanding musical ability, Loving moved up steadily through the ranks, from a private in the infantry to a lieutenant colonel in the Philippine Constabulary. "During the same period, the racism that permeated American society allowed few African Americans to earn Army commissions and even fewer to achieve field rank," Cunningham wrote.

Loving became conductor of the legendary Philippine Constabulary Band, consisting of about eighty Filipino musicians, best known for its performances at Manila's Luneta Park. Years later, Loving came back to Washington to lead the band in a series of performances at William Howard Taft's inauguration. (In fact, the band had been formed during Taft's administration as Philippine governor general at the suggestion of Colonel Henry Allen.) The program included a performance at the White House and at the inauguration parade itself, even in the middle of a blizzard, a moment captured in a photograph preserved at the Library of Congress. "Notwithstanding the members of the band come from a land which is almost tropical, they were astir early yesterday morning and soon on their way through the slush and almost blinding snow to perform their duty in heading the first division that escorted the President-elect from the White House to the Capitol," the *Evening Star* reported. The band also performed at the inauguration of West Potomac Park (see the previous chapter).

The band attracted large crowds in Washington. "That this organization can continue to play to practically capacity audiences week after week in a city not noted for its patronage of band concerts as a rule speaks all that is necessary to demonstrate the sterling musical caliber of this band of native Filipinos," the *Washington Herald* noted. "Long before the hour set for the concert the chair space in the big hall had been exhausted," according to the *Washington Times*. "Late comers stood for an hour and a half during which the program was played and the second floor was crowded from one end of the hall to the other." (A few years later, John Philip Sousa conducted the band as it performed his "Stars and Stripes Forever." "When I closed my eyes," Sousa said later, "I thought it was the U.S. Marine Band playing.")

Loving spent most of the rest of his life in the Philippines. Imprisoned by the Japanese and later placed under house arrest, Loving died in 1945 during the campaign to liberate the Philippines. He was beheaded by the Japanese, according to eyewitness accounts, and his remains have never been found. "Colonel Loving rests somewhere in Philippine soil," Loving's wife, Edith, said at a program at the Luneta in 1952. "Many saw him fall and breathe his last near the Luneta, the place which had been so familiar and so much a part of him."

Dupont Circle and Neighborhood

Alice Roosevelt Home

Alice Roosevelt was the daughter of U.S. President Theodore Roosevelt and lived here, about a block northwest of Dupont Circle. She was outspoken and fiercely independent. The press called her "Princess Alice," and journalists followed her around and quoted everything she said. She was, in many ways, like a modern-day celebrity and was a public figure throughout her lifetime. "Meetings in her drawing room helped to change the course of history," her biographer, Stacy Cordery, wrote, "as she fought successfully to keep the United States from joining the League of Nations in the early 1920s." She would remain a "Washington powerbroker" throughout most of the twentieth century, and "her salon continued to bring together the powerful and the amusing," Cordery wrote. (Embroidered on a pillow in her home: "If you haven't got anything good to say about anyone come and sit by me.") She was, people said, "the other Washington monument."

In 1905, Alice, who was then twenty-one years old, joined a diplomatic mission to Asia. It was a few years after the Spanish-American War, the United States was the world's newest superpower and future U.S. president William Howard Taft—who had just served as governor general in the Philippines and was then Roosevelt's secretary of war—was asked to lead this mission. It was a large diplomatic mission (the largest in history, according to one account), including "seven senators, twenty-three congressmen—together with wives and aides," and Alice. "At the reception at Malacañan, I stood

Residence of Alice Roosevelt, daughter of President Theodore Roosevelt. *Photo by the author.*

for hours with the Wrights and Mr. Taft, all of us literally dripping, while we shook hands with the hundreds of guests," Alice wrote in her memoirs. And just as they did in the United States, members of the press followed Alice overseas and reported on all her adventures, including a marriage proposal that she supposedly received from the sultan of Sulu while she was visiting the Philippines. ("Sultan of Sulu Visits Taft Party and Is Smitten with President's Daughter," according to one headline.)

It turned out to be a big misunderstanding. Upon coming back from her trip, Alice denied many of the fantastic stories told about her. "Neither did I receive any offer of marriage from the Sultan of Sulu," she said. "The circulation of such nonsensical stories is the only outcome of my whole trip that I have to regret." The day the sultan and Alice met, a rival ruler had presented a gift to Alice. Not to be outdone, the sultan of Sulu "tore the ring from his finger and offered it to Miss Roosevelt"—hence the misunderstanding. But Alice did marry the man who actually proposed marriage to her during this same trip to the Philippines—Nicholas Longworth, a member of Congress who later served as U.S. Speaker of the House.

WOODROW WILSON HOUSE

The Woodrow Wilson House was home of President Woodrow Wilson and Edith Wilson after they left the White House in 1921. A small mother-and-child statue called *Pax*, sculpted by Philippine national artist Guillermo Tolentino, is on display here, a gift from Tolentino to President Woodrow Wilson in August 1919.

Tolentino gifted the statue to Wilson at the White House. The story of the meeting between them has been recounted numerous times, including accounts in the *Washington Post* and the *Evening Star* immediately after the meeting, Tolentino's own published recollections published in 1927, a chapter of a book written by artist and art historian Rod Paras Perez in 1976 and more recent articles by historian Ambeth Ocampo. The broad outline is now fairly well known: Tolentino, a young man on an overseas adventure, worked as a waiter at a Rock Creek Park tea house. One of the tea house's frequent customers was First Lady Edith Wilson's secretary, Edith Benham. She knew Tolentino's fledgling artistic skills and had seen *Pax*, Tolentino's homage to Wilson's peace efforts, and helped arrange a meeting between Tolentino and Wilson. "With the statue under my arm...I walked up the White House steps, and was shown into the blue room," Tolentino recalled

The Woodrow Wilson House. *Photo by the author.*

a few years later. Wilson was "greatly pleased" and offered to support Tolentino's plans for further studies. At Wilson's request, his friend Bernard Baruch, a business leader, agreed to become Tolentino's benefactor. He promptly reached out to Tolentino and offered to provide a monthly stipend in support of Tolentino's training, first at *L'Ecole des Beaux Arts* in New York and later in Europe.

What is less known is the unlikely and lifelong friendship between Tolentino and Edith that grew out of this 1919 meeting and their correspondence spanning the following decades. Some of the letters between them from the 1920s appear in a 1973 volume on Tolentino. "The President has your little model in his own room and is very proud of it," Edith Wilson wrote. There are several references to Benham ("You will be interested to know that Miss Benham is married") and to Baruch ("Mr. Baruch has always expressed his great admiration for the spirit of independence you have always shown"). The letters track Tolentino's rising career ("I am delighted to know of the honors which have come to you") and the milestones in their lives ("Your letter of February 29th has touched me very deeply," she wrote to him in 1924, shortly after Wilson died).

In 2021, I helped identify a few letters exchanged between Tolentino and Edith over the 1920–56 period among the Library of Congress's collection that had been previously miscatalogued due to a typo ("Tolentino" versus "Tolention"). The 1956 letter from Tolentino is significant as

The statue *Pax*, a gift from Philippine national artist Guillermo Tolentino to President Woodrow Wilson in August 1919. *Courtesy of the Woodrow Wilson House.*

it is his own account of his life's major artistic achievements ("I will send you a photograph of the said monument to our great hero Andres Bonifacio") and a more personal, and vivid, account of his family life, including about a daughter who had gotten married just days before.

"I have read with real gratification of your life and all you have achieved," Edith wrote in response. The letters in the 1920s were signed, "Faithfully yours." This time she signed it, "Your friend."

CATHEDRAL OF ST. MATTHEW THE APOSTLE

Although the cathedral is probably best known outside D.C. as the site of President John F. Kennedy's funeral mass in 1963—world leaders were here to attend the service, including Diosdado Macapagal, who was then Philippine president and had lived earlier in Washington as a staff member of the immediate postwar Philippine embassy—many memorial masses have been celebrated here in honor of fallen Philippine presidents, including several who died while in office. Commonwealth president Manuel L.

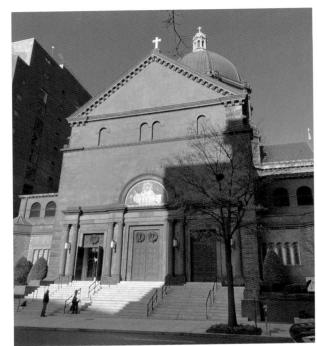

Right: The Cathedral of
St. Matthew the Apostle.
Photo by the author.

Below: Philippine
Commonwealth president
Manuel Quezon's
Funeral Mass at the
Cathedral of St. Matthew
the Apostle. *Courtesy of the
Quezon Family Collection.*

Interior of the Cathedral of St. Matthew the Apostle. *Photo by the author.*

Quezon's funeral mass was held here in August 1944 before his body was temporarily interred at Arlington Cemetery. A memorial mass for postwar Philippine president Manuel Roxas was celebrated in April 1948 by Jesuit priest and historian Father Horacio de la Costa.

In March 1957, about eight hundred people gathered at the cathedral, led by Archbishop Patrick O'Doyle, to mourn the sudden death from an airplane crash of beloved Philippine president Ramon Magsaysay. Among them were U.S. Vice President Richard Nixon, U.S. Chief Justice Earl Warren, House Speaker Sam Rayburn, Senator Millard Tydings (coauthor of the Philippine Independence Act) and "high officials and representatives of the entire Free World diplomatic corps in Washington," according to the *Washington Post*. The United States and the Philippines and "the entire free world have lost a valiant champion of freedom," U.S. President Dwight Eisenhower, who was on official travel at that time, wrote in an official statement.

Magsaysay was only forty-nine years old but "had become the foremost symbol of democracy and the struggle for freedom in Asia," according to the *Washington Post*. He was an "unsophisticated popular hero," the *Post* wrote, who created a complaints center in his office and personally spent time trying to solve countless people's problems—he once personally ended a meeting abruptly and drove one hundred miles to prevent the illegal eviction of a tenant—and, in the process, won his people's trust and

Vintage postcard showing the Hotel 2400, Washington, D.C. *Author's collection.*

affection. He also had personal ties to D.C., as he had visited the city on a few occasions on official business in the immediate postwar period and was much loved by the Philippine community. That week in March 1957, the community and its friends were in mourning. The Philippine embassy was "flooded with messages of condolence," according to the *Post*.

The cathedral has also been the church of many Filipino parishioners over the years. Among them was commonwealth vice-president Sergio Osmeña, who was in D.C. in exile during the Second World War. Osmeña lived a frugal life and walked about a mile from his apartment on 16th Street and Crescent Place—the Hotel 2400, now known as the Envoy Apartments, across the street from Meridian Hill Park—to his office at the Old Philippine Chancery. During this wartime period, marked by shortages of basic commodities and gas rationing, Osmeña declined chauffeur services offered to him, according to his biographer, Vicente Albano Pacis. Each day, on his way to work, he stopped by St. Matthew's Cathedral, "just around the corner on Rhode Island Avenue from the Philippine Building," to hear mass. "He evidently found some solace from hearing mass every morning," Pacis wrote.

CHARLES SUMNER SCHOOL

The Charles Sumner School is a four-story school building located a few blocks southeast of Dupont Circle. It was one of Washington's first schools for African Americans and currently serves as the archival repository of the local public school system. It is also a significant site in the history of Philippine arts, as it hosted a posthumous exhibit of Galo Ocampo's work in the late 1980s.

Ocampo was a leading figure in Philippine arts, best known for the *Brown Madonna*, a pioneering indigenized depiction of the Virgin Mary. In addition, he was a war veteran, a captain in the U.S. Army Forces in the Far East (USAFFE). During the war, he did covert intelligence work tracking Japanese troop movements in Manila and its surrounding areas, serving as art director of a theater group as a cover. In recognition of his military service, his remains are buried at the Arlington Memorial Cemetery.

In the immediate postwar period, he designed the coat of arms of the Philippines, combining Spanish and American symbols—a lion and an eagle, respectively. It was officially adopted on July 3, 1946, one of the final acts of the Philippine Commonwealth prior to independence. Later that year, he came to Washington to formally study heraldry—the design of official symbols—and went on to prepare the original design of the seal of the Philippine president.

He spent the last few years of his life in Arlington, Virginia, a few blocks from St. Ann's Parish, where he and his wife were devout members. They left the Philippines during the martial law period in the Philippines, as he and his wife were "very much concerned about their children's future," according to his sons Mitch and Dennis Ocampo in a 2018 interview. Until Ocampo's death in 1985, he remained as prolific and creative as ever, sometimes painting in multiple rooms. "He would start one in the upstairs bedroom, he would start one on the porch, then started one in the basement," Mitch said.

He also had a small vegetable garden. He planted "giant tomatoes, three-foot-long sitao, ampalaya, snowpeas, and squash," he wrote in a letter to historian Ambeth Ocampo. "God makes my plants grow; I just water them religiously every afternoon," he said.

BATAAN AND CORREGIDOR STREETS

These two streets on opposite sides of Scott Circle are named after two places where important World War II battles took place between, on one side, the Imperial Japanese Army and, on the other side, Philippine and American troops. Some seventy-five thousand Filipino and American soldiers had surrendered at Bataan and were then forced to walk for about one hundred kilometers to a prison camp. By some accounts, about eleven thousand prisoners of war were treated cruelly by their captors and died during this brutal "Death March."

The inauguration took place in 1961, "a perpetual reminder of the gallantry of Philippine and American soldiers who died in the Philippines," according to U.S. Secretary of State Dean Rusk in an address before distinguished guests, including U.S. Chief Justice Earl Warren and Joint Chiefs of Staff General Lyman Lemnitzer. In an editorial he published on that same day, Philippine ambassador Carlos P. Romulo wrote about "those terrible days in 1942" and "the spiritual victory that makes the defeat look puny." "Bataan should always stand as a reminder of the continuing mutuality of Philippine-American friendship," he said.

OLD PHILIPPINE CHANCERY

The Old Chancery of the Philippine embassy, a National Historical Landmark of the Philippines, served as the office of Resident Commissioners Joaquín M. Elizalde and Carlos P. Romulo from 1943 to 1946 and the office of the Philippine Commonwealth Government-in-Exile, led by President Manuel L. Quezon and Vice-President Sergio Osmeña. When the Philippines became independent in 1946, the building became chancery of the Philippine embassy, and today it serves as the consular section of the embassy.

The building is also an important literary site, where members of the first and second generation of Filipino writers in English once worked, including the prize-winning fiction writer Bienvenido N. Santos. "In the fall of 1942, Ben Santos was summoned from his studies at Columbia University and assigned a basement desk in the Information Division of the Commonwealth Building," Leonard Casper wrote in his introduction to an anthology of Santos's fiction. "Santos' own sentiments were fixed on his homeland and the immeasurable distances placed by war between it and not only the Philippine government-in-exile which he served, but also anxious pensionados like himself with endangered families still in the occupied islands." Alongside Santos was the celebrated poet Jose Garcia Villa, one of the best-known poets of his generation. Villa lived and worked in New York for most of his adult life but once worked in this building. "Near Santos worked Jose Garcia Villa," Casper wrote, "mindlessly clipping news items about Bataan and Corregidor while lost in reveries about his first volume of poems, just released: Have Come, Am Here."

In addition, the building is the site of several milestones in Philippine history, two of which include Romulo. On the morning of August 1, 1944, Romulo—who was then secretary of information and public relations of the Commonwealth Government-in-Exile—received news that President Quezon had died. He knocked on the door of Osmeña's office on one of the upper floors of the building. ("For workroom, he was given a tiny room [on] the third floor," Romulo recalled.) When Osmeña opened the door, Romulo said, "Good morning, Mr. President." Osmeña took off his glasses, "wiped them slowly and walked over to the window and looked out," Romulo recalled. "Tears were running down his cheeks." Osmeña asked to be flown to Saranac, New York, where Quezon had died, to personally convey his condolences to Quezon's family, but he was asked to proceed to the Department of Interior instead, where he took his oath of office as the new Philippine Commonwealth president.

Above: Old Philippine Chancery, Washington, D.C. *Photo by the author.*

Opposite, left: The flag of the Philippines at half-mast at the Old Philippine Chancery, Washington, D.C. *Photo by the author.*

Opposite, right: General Carlos Romulo at the Old Philippine Chancery, August 1945. *Press release image from the author's collection.*

In August the following year, in a ceremony held on the second-floor balcony of the building, Romulo—who had served alongside General Douglas MacArthur and President Osmeña at the Battle of Leyte and was now resident commissioner of the Philippine Commonwealth—placed the Philippine flag on its "peacetime" position: blue stripe above, red stripe below. The flag was a personal item—it was a handmade gift from the mother and sister of Captain Harold Shumate, a U.S. soldier from Houston, Texas, who served in the Philippines with the Coast Artillery Corps, became a prisoner of war after the fall of Corregidor and died in prison in August 1942. The flag was prominently displayed in Romulo's office ("the large and beautiful Philippine flag on my wall that was a gift from my friends the Shumate family," he wrote in *My Brother Americans*), and it "accompanied [Romulo] wherever he went," according to newspapers. Throughout his public life, Romulo often spoke movingly of the "blood brotherhood" and deep friendship between Filipinos and Americans. He held a poignant souvenir of that friendship that morning, as a vicious war finally came to an end.

THE WHITE HOUSE AND NEIGHBORHOOD

WHITE HOUSE

The White House has hosted numerous Philippine figures for more than a century, their visits and their official titles reflecting milestones of Philippine history and the transformation of a nation. The White House itself has been shaped by their presence and influence.

Philippine resident commissioners paid courtesy visits to the sitting U.S. president at the beginning of their term and at various points during their temporary residence in D.C. ("On New Year's Day, 1910, the senior Resident Commissioner, Mr. Legarda, took me to wish Happy New Year to President Taft, vice-President James Sherman, and Speaker Joseph G. Gannon," Quezon wrote in his memoirs.) In addition, there are records of visits by members of the Philippine Independence Missions. In June 1922, a large group of Philippine women also visited the White House—the wives and relatives of the official delegates of a Philippine Independence Mission led by Aurora Quezon, the wife of Manuel L. Quezon and the future commonwealth first lady, and Sofia de Veyra, the wife of the resident commissioner (see also the "Foggy Bottom" and "Woodley Park" chapters). They were hosted by First Lady Florence Harding on the South Lawn and came to promote the cause of women's suffrage in the Philippines. Aurora, Sofia and the other members of this delegation, including Pura Villanueva Kalaw, were leaders of the Philippine suffrage movement and were present years later when Philippine Commonwealth

Philippine women with Mrs. Harding on the South Lawn of the White House, 1922. *Library of Congress, Prints and Photographs Division.*

president Manuel Quezon signed the amended Philippine election law, allowing women to vote. From the 1930s on, there are records of visits by Philippine Commonwealth officials and, in the postwar period following Philippine independence, Philippine ambassadors and visiting Philippine officials, including Philippine presidents.

Although many Philippine officials have visited the White House over the years, only President Quezon and his family are known to have spent the night here. They were hosted by President Roosevelt at the White House in May 1942 at the beginning of their exile during the Second World War. They spent the night at the White House, and President Roosevelt hosted a luncheon for them, members of the cabinet and their friends the following day.

In addition to Philippine officials, several important figures in Philippine history and culture have also visited the White House. These include Clemencia López, who met with President Theodore Roosevelt to personally ask for the release of her brothers, associates of the U.S. anti-imperialist movement and who had been arrested at the beginning of the U.S. colonial period in the Philippines; the sultan of Sulu, a powerful

Sergio Osmena, Manuel Quezon and Pedro Guevarra at the White House, 1927. *Library of Congress, Prints and Photographs Division.*

ruler in the southern region of the Philippines; Americans who served as governors general in the Philippines such as Cameron Forbes; the Philippine Constabulary Band, which also performed at the Taft Inauguration; and future Philippine national artist Guillermo Tolentino.

The White House has also been home to many workers from the Philippines. A current chef who joined the White House staff in 2005 is Cristeta Comerford, who is Filipino-American. Beginning in 1909, when newly elected President Taft moved in with his Filipino valet, Monico López Lara, many Filipinos worked as White House stewards, recruited from the U.S. Navy, which has traditionally employed a large number of Filipinos. President Franklin D. Roosevelt, for example, was known to travel with his "Filipino mess boys" who prepared his meals and tended to his needs. ("Much credit is due the President's Filipino mess boys for the success of the dinner this evening," according to the log of the 1943 Tehran conference.)

One of the better-known Filipino stewards is Irineo Esperancilla, who served four U.S. presidents (Hoover, Roosevelt, Truman and Eisenhower) and was, according the *Oakland Tribune*, "a favorite of F.D.R." In 1938, several newspapers reported that Esperancilla had been personally selected by Roosevelt as his "personal chef." He was "a first class cook," according to the *Berkshire Evening Eagle*, and was "master of his trade and a veteran of several presidential cruises," according to a San Francisco press release. In 1959, following his retirement, Esperancilla shared many stories about his life as a steward who was present at key events of the twentieth century. Soviet premier Joseph Stalin declined to eat dishes served at the Tehran Conference, for example, believing that Esperancilla was a Japanese agent.

Presidents had difficulty pronouncing "Irineo." Roosevelt called him "Isaac," which became "Ike" but caused some confusion when Eisenhower moved into the White House. He is also called "Joe the Filipino" in presidential biographies. Truman "was the only President who pronounced my name correctly," Esperancilla recalled.

Finally, the White House itself has seen Philippine touches for more than a century. Visiting Philippine dignitaries have gifted sitting U.S. presidents with Philippine furniture (a dining table made of Philippine mahogany, given to President Truman) and Philippine art (a painting made by Philippine national artist Fernando Amorsolo, given to President Kennedy by Philippine president Macapagal).

In 1909, when Taft became president, First Lady Helen Taft added new features inspired by the years they spent living in the Philippines. "She refurnished many of the rooms with Philippines-style furniture, and had masses of plants and flowers everywhere throughout the White House," wrote Carole Chandler Waldrup in *Wives of American Presidents*. Some called the White House the "Malacanang Palace," after the official residence of the governor general during the U.S. colonial period and later the official residence of the Philippine president in the Commonwealth period.

And where White House fixtures were particularly American, the Tafts missed elements of their Philippine home. Summers at the White House more than a century ago, for example, were particularly uncomfortable. "I wish I had a Filipino sleeping bed for sleeping these nights," President Taft told his wife. "With the mattresses here I wake up a mass of perspiration. Oh for the mats and rattan beds of Manila," he said.

THE BLAIR HOUSE

The Blair House, across from White House on Pennsylvania Avenue, is the U.S. president's official guest house. It has served as a temporary home for several visiting Philippine presidents, including Elpidio Quirino (1949 and 1951), Carlos P. Garcia (1958), Ferdinand Marcos (1966 and 1982) and Corazon Aquino (1989). The signatures of Ferdinand and First Lady Imelda Marcos can be found online in the digitized log book of the guest house.

A Blair House chef wrote for the *Washington Post* and recalled President Aquino's visit. One evening, the president hosted members of the U.S. House and Senate Foreign Relations Committee for dinner. As they ate,

The Blair House. *Photo by the author.*

water began to overflow from a bathtub upstairs and flooded the recently renovated Blair House, upsetting her dinner companions. Aquino laughed and told her guests that it reminded her of the leaky ceilings of her Philippine home during the country's monsoon season—and like many Philippine households, her family placed buckets to collect leaking water. Her amusing story helped put at ease her troubled guests.

BERNARD BARUCH BENCH OF INSPIRATION AT LAFAYETTE PARK

Bernard Baruch is best known in Philippine art history as Guillermo Tolentino's benefactor (see the previous chapter). He was an American business leader who made his fortune in the New York Stock Exchange. The Baruch College of the City University of New York is named after him. He also served as adviser to several U.S. presidents, including President Wilson.

The image here shows his favorite bench—northwest of the General Andrew Jackson statue in Lafayette Square, with a bronze inscription marking the spot—where he sat and waited for his next White House appointment. Baruch's habits were so widely known, according to the National Park Service, that he was sometimes called the "Park Bench Statesman," and a letter was said to have been delivered here marked only "Bernard Baruch, Lafayette Park, Washington, D.C." "There was something comforting in the sight of him sitting cross-legged on a park bench," James Grant wrote, "one pants leg hiked up to reveal an old-fashioned, high-topped black shoe," reportedly purchased from Sears. "Hard candy sometimes rattled in his

Bernard Baruch Bench of Inspiration at Lafayette Park. *Photo by the author.*

pockets," according to Margaret Coit, "but it was for himself, not for the pigeons or the squirrels."

He must have sat here in 1919 just before President Wilson showed him Tolentino's statue, *Pax*, Tolentino's gift to Wilson. "I have seen some of your work, and I am very much interested in it," Baruch wrote to Tolentino soon after Wilson asked him to support Tolentino's art studies in New York. They met and Baruch offered to provide Tolentino a monthly stipend while Tolentino studied at the Beaux-Arts Institute in New York.

They stayed in touch even after Tolentino had moved to Europe for further studies, their letters reflecting Tolentino's artistic evolution and some of the most important events of their time. In 1921, Tolentino wrote to Baruch from Rome and enclosed a photograph of a sketch he made. "The figure is a Sardinian shepherd holding in his hand a mutilated eagle," he explained. "The whole thing represents Sardinia island mutilated in the last world war and aspiring for her independence."

DWIGHT D. EISENHOWER
EXECUTIVE OFFICE BUILDING

The Dwight D. Eisenhower Executive Office Building, also known as the Old Executive Office Building, was constructed to serve the offices of the State Department, the Navy Department and War Department. This building has many ties to the Philippines.

All three departments—State, Navy and War—played key roles in the Spanish-American War, the Battle of Manila Bay and the subsequent acquisition and administration of the Philippines. As a result, many important figures in Philippine-American history once worked here. It was Assistant Secretary of the Navy and future president Theodore Roosevelt, for example, who arranged for George Dewey to lead the Asiatic Squadron. Secretary of State John Hay—after whom a former military facility (now a reservation) in the Philippines is named—helped craft the Treaty of Paris and signed it on behalf of the United States, leading to the annexation of the Philippines. William Howard Taft, after serving as Philippine governor general and prior to becoming U.S. president, served as secretary of war and had an office here.

In addition, elements of the physical structure themselves reflect Philippine ties. The exterior of the North Wing, which was the office of the War Department, displays two Spanish cannons from the Philippines.

Dwight D. Eisenhower Executive Office Building. *Photo by the author.*

George Dewey acquired these brass cannons in May 1898 from the Spanish armory at Cavite, immediately after his victory over the Spanish armada at the Battle of Manila Bay. In addition, General Douglas MacArthur—who led the invasion of Leyte in 1944 and the campaign to liberate the Philippines from the Japanese, among the many roles he played in Philippine history—designed the flowerpots that frame the steps of the building. This was in 1913, when he was a young U.S. Army captain and served as building superintendent of the War Department.

THESE FIVE-INCH BRASS TROPHY GUNS WERE CAPTURED FROM THE SPANISH ARSENAL AT CAVETE, IN THE PHILLIPINE ISLANDS ON MAY 1, 1898, FOLLOWING THE DEFEAT OF THE SPANISH SQUADRON IN MANILA BAY BY THE UNITED STATES NAVY. ADMIRAL DEWEY, THE HERO OF THE CAMPAIGN, DIRECTED THAT THE GUNS BE SENT TO THE UNITED STATES NATIONAL MUSEUM (NOW THE SMITHSONIAN INSTITUTION). THE GUNS ARE ON LOAN FROM THE SMITHSONIAN INSTITUTION DIVISION OF ARMED FORCES HISTORY. PLAQUES ATOP THE GUN BARRELS STATE THEY WERE MADE IN SEVILLA, SPAIN IN 1875.

FROM 1900 UNTIL 1943, THERE WERE 29 SUCH PIECES OF ORDNANCE FROM THE REVOLUTIONARY, MEXICAN-AMERICAN, AND SPANISH-AMERICAN WARS DISPLAYED ON THESE GROUNDS. MANY WERE DISPERSED TO THE BATTLEFIELDS ACROSS THE COUNTRY, WHILE SOME WERE SCRAPPED FOR THE WORLD WAR II EFFORT.

A plaque describing the Spanish-American War cannons, Dwight D. Eisenhower Executive Office Building. *Photo by the author.*

Philippine officials themselves have ties to this building. In 1919, for example, delegates of the first of a series of Philippine Independence Mission led by Manuel L. Quezon, who was then senate president, had their photograph taken in front of this building.

Finally, President Dwight Eisenhower himself, after whom the building is named, spent the 1930s in the Philippines as military adviser to President Quezon. He helped create the first Philippine air corps and fulfilled a lifelong dream of becoming a pilot. He took flying lessons in the Philippines and earned a private pilot's license in 1939 when he was nearly fifty years old. Eisenhower had several flying instructors, including legendary Philippine pilot Jesús Villamor, after whom the headquarters of the Philippine air force is named (see "Georgetown" chapter). Villamor thought that Eisenhower was "a poor pilot but a good student." Eisenhower's son John spent part of his childhood in Baguio in the northern region of Philippines. Just before John died in 2013, he published a book about their life in the Philippines, including his father's flying lessons. "He took great pride in that accomplishment," John wrote.

CORCORAN SCHOOL OF THE ARTS & DESIGN

Trinidad H. Pardo de Tavera was a physician and scholar and among the first group of prominent Filipinos who worked closely with the American colonial government, including as a member of the 1901 Philippine commission. In 1904, he served as president of the St. Louis Exposition's Honorary Board of Commissioners. Also known as the 1904 St. Louis World's Fair, the exposition was a yearlong program to mark the 100th year of the Louisiana Purchase. It featured cultural and technological exhibits, including controversial human exhibits of Philippine minorities (see "Foggy Bottom" chapter).

A reception was held here—then known as the Corcoran Gallery of Art and now GWU's Corcoran School of the Arts & Design—in June 1904 for Trinidad H. Pardo de Tavera. It was hosted by the president of the D.C. Board of Commissioners, Henry B. F. MacFarland. Both MacFarland and Pardo Tavera gave speeches commending "the union of interests between the republic and the archipelago." "We would offer you the traditional freedom of the city," MacFarland told his Filipino guests, "were it not that you already have it as brothers with us under the same flag and shares with us in this center of the national life." Pardo de Tavera, whose parents were Spanish and Filipino, spoke in Spanish, translated into English by an interpreter. Although American and Filipino troops fought during the Philippine-American War, the next war, Pardo de Tavera prophesied, "will be fighting for a common cause as brothers." The American flag, he said, "from now henceforth is also ours."

YMCA (SITE)

West of the White House, just a few steps away on 17th and G Streets, the old YMCA served as the home of the Filipino Club. Local newspaper accounts suggest that the club was active for about half a century in the 1900s in the metro D.C. area and organized many social and cultural programs. The *Washington Post* published an account, for example, of the club's "twelfth annual oratorical contest" held at the YMCA in 1932. "Speaking before a large group of their fellow countrymen and guests at the Y.M.C.A. last night," the *Post* wrote, "six orator members of the club recalled the patriotic endeavors of inhabitants of the islands to establish their independence through legal and martial methods."

In 1924, a young Filipino musician, Francisco Santiago, played the piano at a concert prior to the club's meeting. He played a few classical compositions, including two by Chopin, and accompanied the wife of a Philippine Independence Mission delegate, Mrs. Claro M. Recto ("wife of the minority floor leader in the Philippine house"), who sang a song by Verdi, followed by an English song as an encore.

Santiago had just completed his graduate studies in Chicago months earlier and had performed his compositions at a concert in Chicago in June. He also joined a radio program a month prior and played the same two compositions by Chopin to critical acclaim. A critic singled him out among the members of his graduate class ("the talented composer and pianist from the Philippines"), and another reported that he had "attracted attention." "His execution sounded 'complete' to yours truly," the critic said. "After his work here, he will return to his own land to be a tower of strength to his own people," the *Chicago Evening Post* wrote.

He would, in fact, go on to play a leading role in Philippine music over the next three decades. He taught at the University of the Philippines Conservatory of Music and eventually became its first Filipino director. But his enduring cultural influence was much broader. At a time of growing consciousness of what it meant to be Filipino—what historian Resil Mojares called "concerted Filipinization" during the American colonial period—Santiago, along with fellow composer Nicanor Abelardo, made the kundiman, a genre of Philippine music, more modern and popular. Together, Mojares wrote, they "lifted the kundiman to the status of a national anthem."

Madrillon Restaurant (Site)

The Madrillon was a popular Spanish restaurant in the 1920s and 1930s located at the corner of 15th and New York Streets, just a few steps from the White House. "[M]ovie stars, statesmen, and diplomats" dined here, one newspaper wrote. It was also a favorite among Philippine Commonwealth officials—Quezon "always drops in for many feasts of paella," according to the *Jackson Sun*, and Sergio Osmeña "never failed to order his favorite callos," his biographer wrote.

According to Washington historian John DeFerrari and the *Washington Post*, "Quezon and his determined band of patriots hatched the Philippine independence over the Madrillon's steaming puchero." The puchero is a Spanish stew typically made of chicken, chorizo de Bilbao, garbanzo beans and vegetables simmered in tomato sauce, onions and minced garlic. Peter Borras, the owner of the Madrillon, described it vividly: a "cabalistic piece of cookery," a "gargantuan dish," a "rustic circle of savors" and a "pot which holds life's essentials for rich and poor alike, emblematic of the national wellbeing of a healthy people." "Mother Spain, as well as her Spanish American offspring, feel in unanimity with Santa Teresa who said that 'between the pucheros strolls the Saviour,'" Borras wrote.

In 1934, as Quezon recovered from a gallstone operation at the Johns Hopkins Hospital in Baltimore, he asked his cook to prepare puchero. "When cooked in Baltimore, without the typical chorizos and garbanzos," Borras wrote, it "became a mere New England boiled dinner." Disappointed in his cook's version—which was missing the right chorizos and garbanzos—Quezon sent both his personal physician and his aide-de-camp to Washington to find the essential ingredients. Quezon "had no qualms about what kind of food he wanted," Borras said.

WILLARD INTERCONTINENTAL

Just a few blocks from the White House, the Willard is an iconic hotel that has been a temporary home for many U.S. presidents, including those in Philippine-American history: Taft, Wilson, Coolidge and Harding. Because of its historical significance, it is listed in the National Register of Historic Places. Other important guests include distinguished writers in literature, such as Walt Whitman and Mark Twain. Twain, according to the National Park Service (NPS), completed two volumes at the Willard in the early twentieth century, which would have coincided with the period in which he was a vocal anti-imperialist, advocating strongly for Philippine independence. "I am opposed to having the eagle put its talons on any other land," Twain told the *New York Herald* in 1900. "To the Person Sitting in Darkness" is the title of his essay on imperialism, published the following year.

Many important Philippine occasions took place at the Willard during the first half of the twentieth century, marking milestones of Philippine history. In April 1932, Sergio Osmeña and Manuel Roxas, leaders of a Philippine Independence Mission, hosted a dinner in honor of W. Cameron Forbes, who previously served as governor general of the Philippines (see "National Mall and Capitol Hill" chapter). In February 1938, a program in honor of Paul McNutt, U.S. high commissioner to the Philippines, was held here, featuring a performance by soprano Enya Gonzalez. A short-

Vintage postcard of the Willard Hotel. *Author's collection.*

lived agreement between Osmeña and Roxas on one side and Quezon on the other, who were then political rivals and had conflicting views on a 1933 independence bill, was signed here in April 1933 and is referred to in history books as the Willard Hotel agreement. As Commonwealth vice-president, Osmeña lived here briefly while in exile in 1943 before transferring to an apartment at Hotel 2400 (2400 16th Street, NW).

One particular occasion stands out for its grandeur and significance, marking as it did a turning point in Philippine history. On August 29, 1916, the U.S. Congress passed the Jones Act—led by Virginia congressman William Atkinson Jones, after whom the law was named, and with strong support from Manuel L. Quezon, the Philippine resident commissioner. Although Quezon was the nonvoting Philippine representative in U.S. Congress, his political skills were legendary (the *Washington Times* wrote approvingly of his persuasive "political talents of wide variety and high order"). The Jones Law was a landmark legislation that pledged to recognize Philippine independence, created a freely elected bicameral Philippine legislature and—under Governor General Francis Burton Harrison—subsequently led to the accelerated integration of Filipinos into the civil service.

To mark the occasion, Quezon hosted a grand banquet at the Red Room of the New Willard to celebrate the passage of the Jones Law and to thank Jones. Because he was leaving the following day after seven years in Washington, it also became Quezon's farewell to Congress and his own grand sendoff ("that which he thoughtfully intended to make an appreciation of Congress and Mr. Jones, 'Father of the Bill,' was turned into a tribute to his own worth, his own splendid work," Patrick Gallagher wrote for the *Philippine Review*). "The table occupied the full length of this spacious chamber," Gallagher said. "It was banked by the pick of the flowers that bloom at this season of the year in Washington"—gladiolas, magnolias and roses. Quezon gave Jones a silver cup as a token of gratitude (the cup is preserved at the Jones ancestral home in Warsaw, Virginia), and members of Congress gifted Quezon with a gold watch ("in appreciation of his splendid services in the cause of Philippine independence," the dedication said). About one hundred guests were served an elaborate meal, including *Supreme de Volaille Perigeux* and *Pommes de Terre Lorette*; ham; salads; and dessert, *Mousse de Peche* and *Friandises*.

The next day, Quezon left Washington and "returned to Manila a real popular hero," Francis Burton Harrison wrote. "A typhoon was blowing in the bay, my ship was detained," Quezon recalled, "and in the pouring rain the old and the young alike, including children, stood for hours, waiting to cheer me when I landed." A Filipino poet, Fernando Ma. Guerrero, wrote a sonnet—"inscribed in a silver hatchet"—in his honor. "Girls in pink showered him with flowers," Stanley Karnow wrote. "He received ovations on all sides," Harrison said.

"Without making a campaign," Quezon wrote, "I was elected Senator by unanimous vote from my district." Quezon soon after was elected the first president of the newly created senate. "Mr. Quezon thus receives at the hands of his own people a distinction that indicates that they accord to him the same recognition that was extended in this country," the *Washington Times* wrote, "for his services in behalf of their aspiration to autonomous government." "There are enthusiastic admirers who compare this young man to Alexander Hamilton," the *Washington Times* added, "and predict for him a career whose highest eminences have not yet nearly been reached."

Thirty more years would pass—two world wars, a global economic depression, a Japanese occupation, a massive military campaign to liberate the Philippines and a total of five more U.S. presidents—before the Philippines finally became a sovereign nation. And although Quezon would eventually become president of the Philippine Commonwealth, he did not live long enough to see his country's independence.

But in August 1916 at the Willard, Quezon—only thirty-eight years old, at the cusp of an extraordinary political career—celebrated the extraordinary progress he and his colleagues had made toward Philippine independence.

Downtown Washington

The Metropolitan Club

The Metropolitan Club is a private membership cub that has been around since the 1860s. Its home is at the corner of 17th and H Streets. According to its own literature, its "proximity to the White House and other icons of the nation's capital has made it a destination for many local, national and international leaders, including nearly every U.S. President since Abraham Lincoln."

Among its members in the late 1890s was George Dewey, who lived in the Everett next door to the club on H Street when he was in his sixties, semi-retired and a member of the Lighthouse Board. His friend and fellow Metropolitan Club member Theodore Roosevelt, who was then assistant secretary of the navy, arranged for him to lead the Asiatic Squadron. Dewey traveled to Hong Kong, prepared for war and then on May 1, 1898, defeated the Spanish Armada at the Battle of Manila Bay. That decisive victory made the United States the world's newest superpower, and Dewey came back a conquering hero. There were parades in his honor and memorabilia bearing his name or likeness; a D.C. building was named after his flagship the USS *Olympia*, and he was later made admiral of the navy.

But before this rise to fame, for many years in the 1890s, he had a quiet routine in Washington, according to his biographer. He lived on the third floor of the Everett, and he preferred to walk up the stairs rather than take the elevator. Around eight o'clock each morning, he ate the same breakfast meal

The Metropolitan Club, 1922. *Library of Congress, Prints and Photographs Division.*

(consisting of "fruit, a couple of 'medium' boiled eggs, orange marmalade, and corn muffins"). He then walked over to the club next door to read books, play chess or spend time with his friends.

DEPARTMENT OF VETERANS AFFAIRS (SITE OF THE ARLINGTON HOTEL)

The Arlington Hotel, a luxury hotel of the late 1800s once stood on this site, at the corner of 15th Street and Vermont Avenue. It was "the most opulent of the great post–Civil War hotels," historian James M. Goode said, the "successful wedding of a severe Anglo-Italianate façade, with a curved mansard reminiscent of the New Louvre in Paris." It hosted European monarchies as well as Washington's financial and political elite. Two important figures in Philippine history stayed here for a few days during their visit to Washington. In early 1899, Philippine lawyer Felipe Agoncillo, the first Filipino diplomat according to his biography, and Juan Luna, the Filipino artist best known for his prize-winning mural *The Spoliarium*, were in

Above: Arlington Hotel, circa 1880–89. *Library of Congress, Prints and Photographs Division.*

Right: Arlington Hotel, circa 1901. *Library of Congress, Prints and Photographs Division.*

Washington to stop the U.S. Senate from ratifying the Treaty of Paris—signed the previous month by the United States and Spain—and to prevent the U.S. annexation of the Philippines.

A Secret Service member assigned to follow Agoncillo and Luna was interviewed by the *Washington Post* and provided an account of the Philippine delegation's habits: "[At] about 10 o'clock every morning, a Secret Service man may be seen…somewhere in sight of the public exit of the Arlington Hotel. He doesn't need to be on hand any sooner, because the Philippine legation does not come out until that time."

Agoncillo and Luna stayed for a few days, unable to secure an audience with any U.S. legislative or executive official, despite writing multiple letters to Secretary of State John Hay. Meanwhile, back in the Philippines, a Nebraskan volunteer, William Grayson, fired a shot the evening of February 4, 1899—it is not clear whether he killed anyone—sparking the beginning of the Philippine-American War. The U.S. Senate ratified the Treaty of Paris two days later, and Agoncillo and Luna—now "subject to temporary arrest," according to Agoncillo's biographer, because the two countries were at war—quietly left Washington. "I've worked for our beloved country with unfailing courage and devotion," he later told his wife, Marcela, "but I return bitterly disappointed at the refusal of our American ally to recognize the independence of our country." The war would range on for three years, officially ending in 1902, at the enormous cost of over 4,000 Americans lives, 20,000 Filipino combatants and close to 200,000 civilians who "may have died from famine and various other causes, including atrocities committed by both sides," according to one estimate.

Some years later, the hotel was demolished, and in its place, a new building was constructed that is now the U.S. Department of Veterans Affairs building. In the 1920s, in room 217, one of the officials who worked here in the Judge Advocate General's Office was Lieutenant Dennis Quinlan, who had previously served in the Philippines, including during the years of the Philippine-American War.

There is a particularly moving account of Quinlan's military service, although Isagani Giron, a local Philippine historian, has contested details of this narrative. At the Battle of Tirad Pass, a key battleground of the Philippine-American War, the young general Gregorio del Pilar—otherwise known as the "Boy General," as he was only in his early twenties—and about sixty Filipino men fought bravely against several hundred well-armed U.S. soldiers led by Major Peyton March, who later served during the First

World War as the army chief of staff (see "Metro D.C. Region" chapter). Del Pilar supposedly knew that it was essentially a suicide mission, with the aim of allowing General Emilio Aguinaldo enough time to escape. Del Pilar died in battle and was stripped of his clothes and a few personal possessions, including his diary, a gold locket and a woman's handkerchief. His naked cadaver was left unburied until Lieutenant Dennis Quinlan and his troops came along and gave del Pilar a proper burial. "An officer and a gentleman," he wrote on the young general's tombstone.

ARMY AND NAVY CLUB

The Army and Navy Club is another private membership club in Washington, with most of its members consisting of retired and active military personnel. Its home is on the corner of 17th and I Streets, on the southwest corner of Farragut Square.

The building has several ties to Philippine-American history dating back to the early colonial period. Admiral George Dewey himself was a member of the Army and Navy Club. In addition, the club owns an oil painting of the Battle of Manila Bay made in 1899 by Spanish artist Alfonso Sanz—a Spanish naval medical officer and a member of the Spanish Royal Academy of Arts—who was captured by the Americans. "The painting…is regarded as an accurate depiction of Dewey's victory over the Spanish fleet," according to the notes accompanying the painting.

The club building is home to the Military Order of the Carabao, an association of military personnel created in jest during the Philippine-American War that has since survived for more than one hundred years. The order began as a tongue-in-cheek response to the pretentiously named Military Order of the Dragon, created by those who had served in China. However, some have been critical of its origins and its rituals, including song lyrics thought to be racist. ("The historic songs do reflect a racism prevalent in the military and in society at large at the beginning of the 20th century," one affiliate said, although he joined a program and "saw absolutely no evidence that such attitudes toward Filipinos exist.") The Order still meets regularly in this building.

In June 1904, a reception for visiting Philippine officials took place in this building, part of an elaborate program including a luncheon at the White House. At the club, Secretary of War Taft along with local U.S. officials hosted the large Philippine delegation of about fifty Filipinos, led by

prominent politicians, scholars and revolutionary figures including Trinidad Pardo de Tavera and Benito Legarda.

Among them was Mariano Trias, the revolutionary general who had served in Aguinaldo's cabinet and led Philippine troops in Cavite, "the hotbed of the revolution," according to the *Evening Star*. Trias said nothing for most of the following day but, by his powerful presence, seemed to intimidate those around him. "He seemed to retire within himself," the *Evening Star* wrote, "after the manner of Napoleon." When asked about the general, his companions spoke in hushed tones ("lowered their voice to a whisper"), "*El general habla poco*" ("The general speaks little").

Finally, Trias spoke. "*Americanos mi(s) amigos,*" he said.

Opposite: The Army and Navy Club, circa 1900–1906. *Library of Congress, Prints and Photographs Division.*

Above: The Army and Navy Club. *Photo by the author.*

THE ORME BUILDING

As the Philippine-American War ended and American officials accelerated Philippine nation-building efforts, Filipinos were recruited and appointed to offices of the U.S. colonial administration.

In 1909, on Christmas Eve, Manuel L. Quezon arrived in D.C. to become the newest Philippine resident commissioner—a nonvoting member of U.S. Congress representing the Philippines—and serve alongside the more senior statesman, Benito Legarda. (Quezon had visited the United States a few years before and caused a minor controversy when he quoted Theodore Roosevelt without permission.) Quezon spent Christmas Eve inside this building on 14th and K Streets, his home for the next few years—then known as the Champlain Apartment House, now known as the Orme Building. On Christmas Day, by his own account in his posthumously published autobiography, he went out wearing "fur-lined

Left: Champlain Apartment, 1424 K Street. The building—now known as the Orme Building—was the 1909 residence of Resident Commissioners Manuel Quezon and Benito Legarda. Nicolas Tiongson is shown leading a walking tour nearby in 2018. *Photo by the author.*

Opposite: Champlain Apartment, 1424 K Street, circa 1918. *Library of Congress, Prints and Photographs Division.*

gloves" and a "fur overcoat" and walked along the city's snow-covered streets. (Newspapers published the following day included accounts of a blizzard that hit Washington and the East Coast region.) Quezon walked around briefly before quickly rushing back to his apartment, fearful that he "would lose his ears" from the cold.

FOGGY BOTTOM

GEORGE WASHINGTON UNIVERSITY

There are numerous links between George Washington University (GWU), which occupies a large portion of the Foggy Bottom neighborhood, and Philippine history—including American graduates who served in the U.S. colonial government, Filipino students who played prominent roles in Philippine history and government and even specific buildings in which important events took place.

One of the first and youngest civilian officials in the American colonial government was a graduate of George Washington University (GWU). W. Morgan Shuster served first as a Philippine customs officer, then as secretary of public instruction and finally as member of the Philippine Commission in the early 1900s, in quick successive rounds of promotion owing to his outstanding performance. Although he was an early supporter of the U.S. colonial enterprise in the Philippines, remarkably—after a brief but controversial stint as head of Iran's treasury, during which time he had "come to doubt whether it is ever wise for people to govern another"—he later became one of the strongest supporters of Philippine independence. At a Philippine banquet at the Raleigh Hotel in 1913, he announced that "the Filipinos were now in a position to run their own government and become an independent nation." He "aroused the banqueters to enthusiasm," the *Washington Times* wrote. He became president of the Century Company, a publishing firm, and published many important volumes written by

Philippine authors, including *The Good Fight*, the posthumously published autobiography of his good friend and future Philippine Commonwealth president Manuel L. Quezon.

Many of the city's first Filipino residents were GWU students on government scholarships, also known as *pensionados*, who were then expected to return to the Philippines upon completing their studies. It was, in many ways, a forerunner of the U.S. Fulbright scholarship program. There have been many Filipino GWU students over the years, including Hadji Gulamu Rasul of Jolo, who was a student in the 1920s and who—unusual for that period—married Alma Stewart, a member of a prominent family in Virginia, and later became a member of Philippine Congress. Helena Benitez, a distinguished 1939 GWU graduate whose portrait is displayed in the lobby of the School of Education and Human Development (2134 G Street NW), served as Philippine senator and spent many years in global public service, including as chair of the UN Commission on the Status of Women (1969) and the first woman to serve as president of the UN Environment Program Governing Council (1975). She was also founder of the Bayanihan Philippine Dance Company and for many years served as chair of the board of the trustees of the Philippine Women's University, a school founded by her parents.

Corcoran Hall at George Washington University (GWU). Here, the Philippine debate team defeated the GWU team in April 1928. *Photo by the author.*

Another student was Jose Abad Santos, a law graduate student in 1909 who is also thought by some to have been the first president of Filipino Student Association in D.C. Abad Santos later moved back to the Philippines and eventually became the fifth Supreme Court chief justice of the Philippines. In 1942, as members of the Commonwealth cabinet left the Philippines to go in exile in the United States, Abad Santos left in charge of the Philippine government and was subsequently arrested by the Japanese. Refusing to cooperate with them, Abad Santos was sentenced to die.

This story appears in several accounts of his life, based on the recollections of a Japanese interpreter present. As Abad Santos was being led to his execution, his young son, Pepito, who was with him, started crying. Abad Santos asked Pepito to stop crying and to show the Japanese soldiers that it was a privilege to die for one's country. GWU president Cloyd Marvin posthumously awarded Santos a special citation in 1958, in recognition of his heroism.

At GWU's Corcoran Hall, a debate took place in April 1928 between the debate teams of the university of the Philippines (UP) and GWU ("Resolved, that the Philippine Islands should be granted immediate and complete independence"). The Philippine team won, its fifth successive victory after defeating Stanford, California, Utah and Colorado. The team would go undefeated against a total of fourteen universities, including Cornell and Harvard. The team was coached by future general and diplomat Carlos P. Romulo, who was then a young journalist and a lecturer at the University of the Philippines. "We returned to Manila and were given a dazzling reception at the pier," Romulo wrote in his memoirs.

THE MONROE HOUSE

The Arts Club of Washington is a private membership club of artists and professionals. Founded in 1916, its home is the Monroe House on I Street between 20th and 21st Streets where U.S. President James Monroe lived in the 1800s.

Known as a progressive club that was first in Washington to admit women into its membership, the club has also hosted members of the Philippine community beginning in its early days. In October 1921, for example, Sofia de Veyra was a guest speaker to launch that season's "fortnightly salons." Here in Washington, as the wife of resident commissioner Jaime de Veyra, Sofia educated Americans about her country (see "Woodley Park" chapter). At the Monroe House, she gave a presentation and, together with another guest, displayed "hand-wrought silver, jewelry, fabrics, paintings and other specimens of Philippine handiwork," according to the *Washington Post*.

Juan Arellano—best known as the architect of the Manila Central Post Office, the Jones Bridge and other Philippine landmarks—displayed his watercolors here in January 1927. His watercolors are much lesser known than his architecture, and he himself said that he painted only as a form of "relaxation from his real work as an architect."

The Monroe House, circa 1937. *Library of Congress, Prints and Photographs Division.*

"Wild Man of 1907 Comes Back to U.S. as Noted Architect," the *Washington Post* announced just weeks prior to his exhibit. Arellano had been a human exhibit at the 1907 Jamestown Fair, a live display of one of the subjects of America's new colonial enterprise and the beneficiary of its civilizing mission, much like the shameful and racist human displays at the 1904 St. Louis World's Fair. And notwithstanding the strong sentiments against such displays and efforts to end them, this practice would persist for many more decades until 1958, according to Jose Fermin, author of a book on the 1904 fair.

"For seven months he wore a pineapple-fiber shirt and allowed himself to be ogled," historian Daniel Immerwahr wrote in 2019. For his "work," he earned enough money (about twenty dollars per month, according to one account) to study art and architecture in Philadelphia, first at the Pennsylvania Academy of Arts and then at the Drexel Institute and the University of Pennsylvania.

Arellano later became one of the Philippines' most important architects, was nominated to design the UN headquarters and designed some of the enduring structures of prewar Manila, including the Metropolitan Theater, renovated in 2021. There is a sense, as others have suggested, that the first encounters between the broader American public and Filipinos were a form of theater, an empire's display of its civilizing mission. At Jamestown, the young Arellano had been displayed as a human exhibit—some would say he was displayed as a "savage"—an educated Filipino playing a part in a public performance, yet to discover his immense artistic gifts that would someday create a national theater.

His watercolors at the Monroe House in 1927 won much praise from the *Washington Post*'s art critic. "There is an uplift about them that is quite irresistible," the critic wrote. "One has the feeling that Arellano paints for the love of it; nothing is labored or forced."

THE MANILA HOUSE

This neighborhood also includes the Manila House, on 24th and K Streets, the first center of community life among Filipino immigrants from the 1930s on. A Philippine community association, the Visayan Circle, purchased the building in the late 1930s, and it quickly became the center of social life through the 1950s—here is where they met and spent time with fellow members of the community, shared Philippine meals and played Philippine music. A member of the parish that now owns the building recalls a row

Right: The Manila House. *Photo by the author.*

Below: Juliana Panganiban, Rudy Panganiban and three other men outside of Manila House, circa spring 1944. *Courtesy of Rita Cacas and the Rita M. Cacas Filipino American Community Archives in the University of Maryland Libraries Special Collections.*

The Manila House marker, indicating that it is an ALA Literary Landmark. *Photo by the author.*

of taxicabs—many Filipinos worked as taxi drivers in the postwar period—outside the building.

Occasionally, members of the Philippine community gambled or became rowdy and found themselves in trouble with the D.C. police. In 1951, for example, dozens of people were arrested for "disorderly conduct." There is one amusing story about the Manila House told by a local police captain, a Captain Blick. At the time, "Paul Jones" was the name of a popular mixer dance—at a signal (a whistle or someone shouting "Paul Jones"), people switched partners, just as they do when square dancing. Blick told the *Evening Star* that he had once raided the Manila House "on a night when a dance was in progress upstairs." "He said when he entered he blew his whistle," the *Evening Star* reported, "and the dancers above thought a Paul Jones was in progress and started changing partners."

A few years ago, my family and I worked with members of the Philippine community to have the building recognized by the American Library Association as a literary landmark—one of a handful of literary landmarks in Washington, together with the Library of Congress—thanks to the stories set at the Manila House written by Bienvenido N. Santos, an American Book Award winner who first came to the United States as a government scholar and became a D.C. resident during the war while working for the Commonwealth Government-in-Exile (see "Dupont Circle and Neighborhood" chapter).

The Elise Apartment

One Foggy Bottom resident in the postwar period was Josefina Guerrero, also known as Joey Guerrero Leaumax, a woman who served as a spy in the Philippines during the Second World War. In her later life, following retirement, she became a Kennedy Center usher and lived in the Elise

The Elyse Apartment, former residence of Josephine Guerrero. *Photo by the author.*

Apartment on New Hampshire Avenue in this neighborhood. She was a member of the St. Stephen Martyr Catholic Church just steps away.

"She'd dress in a black skirt and plain white blouse and pull on a long coat and slip out of her apartment on New Hampshire Avenue and walk a few blocks in the fading sun to the grand John F. Kennedy Center for the Performing Arts, on the east bank of the Potomac, where she was Joey Leaumax, usher, volunteer," according to her biographer, Ben Montgomery, who wrote *Leper Spy: The Story of an Unlikely Hero of World War II.*

Few members of her Foggy Bottom community would have known her origins as a spy. As a young woman, she contracted leprosy. Instead of being incapacitated, she used it to do covert work during the Second World War undisturbed, as people shied away from her. According to *TIME* magazine, "No sentry detained her for long after he had discovered, beneath her thin blouse and the swathed bandages, the lesions of leprosy." In one terrifying episode described in Montgomery's book, Guerrero walked dozens of miles through enemy territory to personally hand over to American troops a map of Japanese mines ("traps on the north side of Manila" and a new mine field "east of Blumentritt"). The map, sketched by Filipino guerrillas, was attached "between her shoulder blades over the leprous pox that had spread to her neck and face, and arms," Montgomery wrote. It was considered a suicide mission. "You had better go to confession and make a good act of contrition," someone told her, "for you will not be coming back." But she did survive and is thought to have saved countless Filipinos and Americans. President Harry Truman awarded her the Medal of Freedom.

After the war, she studied English at San Francisco State University and Spanish at Middlebury College. She served as a Peace Corps volunteer in El Salvador, Colombia and Niger. She was an advocate for lepers. But just as she carried out her wartime work quietly, she chose to live in anonymity in her later years, Montgomery said, and died in obscurity in 1996. "Joey Guerrero Leaumax, Kennedy Center Usher," her obituary simply said.

"I want to be a good soldier," she once told a friend. According to Montgomery, she was convinced that "even the lowliest could be a vessel, could be of service to the greater good."

Georgetown

M Street

M Street is a historic row of shops, bars and restaurants located near the Potomac River in the Georgetown neighborhood of D.C. One neighborhood guide indicates that Georgetown has close to "2.1 million square feet of retail space" and more than four hundred shops and restaurants, with M Street as the center of this shopping district and residential neighborhood. More than 7 million people visit Georgetown each year, and on weekends M Street is particularly vibrant and bustling with social and retail activities.

In March 1912, however, the street took a more somber tone. Thousands of people quietly lined M Street to watch a funeral procession bearing the remains of those killed in the mysterious explosion of the USS *Maine*. A few hundred people—the estimates vary from 260 to more than 300 sailors—died when the battleship USS *Maine* suddenly exploded and sank while anchored in Havana fourteen years earlier, in February 1898. "Remember the *Maine*, to Hell with Spain!" became the rallying cry as the American publicly blamed Spain for this disaster. Two months later, the United States declared war against Spain, and the histories of the United States and the Philippines have been entwined since then.

The remains of some 150 American sailors—the actual number is disputed—were buried in Arlington in December 1899, and dozens more were recovered in 1912 and were given a military burial one afternoon in March that year. A memorial ceremony led by President Taft took place

USS *Maine* Memorial and the graves of the victims of the USS *Maine* explosion, circa 2001, Arlington National Cemetery. *Library of Congress, Prints and Photographs Division.*

on the south side of the State, War and Navy Department Building. From there, they marched to Arlington, "via 17th street, to Pennsylvania Avenue, on the avenue to Aqueduct bridge," according to the *Evening Star*. The Aqueduct Bridge linked Georgetown to Rosslyn prior to the construction of Key Bridge.

"The bodies of the martyrs of the Maine sixty-seven sailors of lost identity, enwrapped in caskets marked 'unknown', although they died as nobly as an admiral might, are the sacred objects of a nation's homage today," the *Washington Times* wrote. A photograph of the procession on M Street in front of the Key Mansion is preserved in the Library of Congress.

GEORGETOWN UNIVERSITY

Georgetown University is a private academic institution administered by Jesuit priests and lay leaders. The university has numerous ties to the Philippines beginning with Georgetown faculty and graduates who were among the first to join the U.S. colonial administration in the Philippines. Several members of the first generation of Philippine government scholars, such as Maximo Kalaw, as well as some of the first Filipino Jesuits and American Jesuits who served in the Philippines, were trained at Georgetown University. In particular, several Filipino and American Jesuits were trained at Woodstock College (a Jesuit seminary in Woodstock, Maryland,

Georgetown University. *Photo by the author.*

that existed until about 1969, the archives of which are now preserved at Georgetown's Lauinger Library) and at Georgetown University, prior to their ordination. Some of them were ordained at the university chapel, such as Joseph Mulry in 1921 and Agustin Consunji in 1925. Future Philippine president Gloria Macapagal Arroyo was a student in the 1960s and, according to student newspaper *The Hoya*, had a higher GPA than her classmate and future U.S. President William Jefferson Clinton.

GASTON HALL AND CARROLL PARLOR

On April 17, 1937, Georgetown University awarded Commonwealth President Manuel L. Quezon an honorary doctor of laws degree, along with two Georgetown professors, D. Percy Hickling and Charles Albert Keigwin. Coinciding with the university's annual celebration of Founders' Day, the ceremony began at 8:30 p.m. and took place at the distinguished Gaston Hall "before 800 dignitaries," an article said, including European ministers, diplomats, Catholic officials and, among the Philippine guests, Resident Commissioner Quentin Paredes, Conrado Benitez and Helena Benitez (see "Foggy Bottom" chapter), Sofia de Veyra (see "Foggy Bottom" and "Woodley Park" chapters) and many others. The Quezon family sat on the front row, "pleased

Old Philippine school seal on display at Georgetown University's Gaston Hall. *Photo by the author.*

and happy," the *Evening Star* said. "There were the young Misses Aurora and Zeneida," the paper added, "and the diminutive Manuel Quezon, Jr., who arrived for the evening's celebration in a natty English top hat of shiny silk." A reception followed in the Carroll Parlor of Healy Hall.

"To the solemn note of a chapel bell taken from the St. Mary's Church, the first English Catholic Church in North America," the university president, Arthur O'Leary, SJ, said while conferring the degree on Quezon, citing Quezon's lifelong advocacy for Philippine independence. Quezon, a document accompanying the degree stated, "has shown in word and unsparing self-sacrifice a noble ambition to build a traditionally Christian people into a nation unshakably supported by the strong girders of social justice and securely founded on the bedrock of peaceful perpetuity, the

The Carroll Parlor at Georgetown University. *Photo by the author.*

law of Christ, and thus to present to nations of the world an excellent and imitable model of a happy and prosperous modern state."

In accepting the honorary degree, Quezon said, "I take it not so much as the measure of your appraisal of my worth as an individual and a public servant, but rather as an evidence of your conviction that the cause in the service of which I have devoted my life is a just and a noble one. More than this, to me this distinction which I am receiving from your hands means that in the estimation of Georgetown University, the Filipino people have attained the dignity of nationhood and have deservedly won their right to self-determination." He rejected "war as an instrument of national policy" and vowed "never to resort to arms except in defense of our country."

Some years later, in late 1942, while Quezon and his family were in exile in D.C. during the war, Quezon wrote a letter to O'Leary. He thanked him for sending a Georgetown ROTC contingent to a mass celebrating the anniversary of the Commonwealth—adding "color and dignity to the occasion." Quezon also looked back on the honorary doctorate the university conferred on him. "I am happy to think," Quezon told O'Leary, "that I am thanking an old friend of mine." He wrote by hand on the lower margin, "This is a belated letter but I have been ill." He died nearly two years later. Tuberculosis "afflicted him for many years," Georgetown's *The Hoya* said, and finally "claimed the life of this courageous, proud, and kindly statesman and scholar." He died in exile, never seeing the war's end, nor his country's complete independence.

ALEXANDER GRAHAM BELL AND THE VOLTA LABORATORY

Alexander Graham Bell is known as the inventor of the telephone. He was also the co-founder of AT&T and conducted path-breaking research in optical telecommunications, hydrofoils and aeronautics. His wife, Mabel, was deaf, and it is safe to assume that she had a deep influence on his research. The Volta bureau was his laboratory in D.C. for sound experiments, named after Alessandro Volta and the Volta prize that he won from the French government after inventing the telephone.

Although we do not normally associate Bell with the Philippines, he became president of the National Geographic Society from 1898 to 1903, critical years in U.S. history, including the Spanish-American War, U.S. victory and the annexation of the Philippines and the early years of the American colonial government in the Philippines. And *National Geographic* played an influential role in shaping the public conversation on the U.S. imperial project in the Philippines, according to Julia A. Tuason, first framed as one of "economic exploitation" and then eventually one of "moral responsibility."

Volta Bureau, circa 1969. *Library of Congress, Prints and Photographs Division.*

Not surprisingly, the Philippines appeared frequently in Bell family correspondence, reflecting critical moments early in Philippine-American history. One letter from Mabel to Alexander ("Alec") written shortly after the Battle of Manila Bay in May 1898 echoes an opinion published in a British paper. "He says no one can tell, but, sending 20,000 soldiers and the Monterey to the Philippines doesn't look like giving it up," she wrote. A letter from Alexander written at the Volta laboratory in March 1901 described a lecture he had attended about India. "A large audience was present which evidently realized that we can learn from India what to do with the Philippines," he said.

GEORGETOWN UNIVERSITY HOSPITAL

At least two remarkable Filipinos died here at the Georgetown University hospital. They could not have been more different—one was a priest, after whom the Jesuit Pre-Novitiate in the Philippines is named, and the other was a military pilot, after whom the Philippine air force headquarters is named. But both fought valiantly during the Second World War, and their entwined lives led them to Washington in the postwar period.

Teddy Arvisu

Teddy Arvisu, SJ, was an outstanding student at the prewar Ateneo and was the valedictorian of his class. When he turned twenty-one in mid-1941, he entered the Sacred Heart Novitiate, to prepare to become a Jesuit priest. His parents were against it ("His father…was said to be hoping that his son would marry one of Quezon's daughters," his friend and fellow Jesuit Miguel Bernad recalled) and sued Teddy to force him to leave the novitiate. After losing their court case, his parents, with President Quezon's intervention, arranged for Teddy to be drafted into the army. John Hurley, SJ, who was head of the Philippine Jesuits, made plans to fly to Baguio with Teddy in early December to meet with President Quezon and "discuss our little problem." "When we arrived at the airport, we found a scene of great agitation," Father Hurley said—the Japanese had just attacked Pearl Harbor. A few months later, Teddy was a third lieutenant in the Philippine army, defending Bataan alongside his Ateneo classmates.

Teddy survived Bataan, the Death March and the rest of the Second World War, including a period of serious illness. In 1952, he was ordained at Woodstock College, an old Jesuit seminary in Maryland. He reconciled with his parents, Bernad recalled, and Teddy's father served at his first mass. An entry in Teddy's diary, written a week after ordination, described "a surge of desire to be holy," a longing to "yield to this grace"—"before familiarity allows us to build resistance to this summoning and challenging grace."

Several years later, Teddy suffered a brain tumor and lost the ability to speak after surgery. He could only one say one word near the end of his life, Bernad recalled: "Guess." ("But there was no way of guessing what he had in in mind," Bernad said.) Teddy died at the Georgetown University Hospital in 1957.

Few would remember Teddy's military service. "With a telephone in one hand and a rifle in the other, Arvisu held off the Japanese until he at last succeeded in bringing up the reinforcements necessary to repel the Japanese at that particular point," General Carlos P. Romulo recalled. "Arvisu fought like a tiger," he said. But Teddy himself never talked about Bataan, nor the military medals he received "for gallantry in action." "In his modesty he never spoke of that, and rarely of the Death March," his classmate John Carroll, SJ, said.

Felipe Buencamino, who served with Teddy in Bataan, wrote in his diary about the morning of their surrender. "We were ordered to stack our guns and disarm," he wrote. "The white flag was raised on top of the highest hill. All Filipino troops in Bataan were going to surrender together." Some of his companions seemed relieved, he said. "They were glad the fighting was over, no matter how it ended." Teddy, he said, was crying.

Jesús Villamor

Jesús Villamor was a distinguished World War II pilot. He served as captain in the U.S. Army Forces in the Far East during the war. During the Japanese occupation, he worked with American and Filipino guerrillas and created an intelligence network that enabled General Douglas MacArthur's Leyte invasion and the subsequent liberation of the Philippines. In the postwar period, he served briefly in the Civilian Aeronautics Administration and then later joined the U.S. Air Force, where he was promoted to colonel. After leaving the U.S. Air Force, he worked as consultant to private firms on aviation affairs in the Southeast Asian region. He died at the Georgetown University Hospital in 1971, following a bout with a lung tumor and pneumonia.

Villamor is probably best remembered for two heroic aerial battles at the beginning of the war while flying an "antiquated" P-26 "Peashooter" against superior enemy planes. He received the Distinguished Service Cross twice. The December 10 award cited his "courage and leadership at great personal hazard" as he led "three pursuit planes into action against attacking

Japanese planes." The December 12 award noted that "Captain Villamor led six pursuit planes against 54 Japanese bombers," and one enemy plane was "destroyed by fire from Captain Villamor's plane." MacArthur commended the "six Filipino pilots" who were "undaunted by the tremendous odds against them."

Villamor and his pilots displayed "unbelievable courage," MacArthur said. One of Villamor's fellow pilots, Geronimo Aclan, "jerking his plane wildly," rushed inexplicably toward an incoming enemy warplane, missing by just a few inches. Another pilot, Jose Gozar, who was a member of another squadron and happened to be present that day, "rushed into an unmanned plane and had flown straight into the fray."

Moments after their shocking victory on December 10 and as soon as Villamor landed, a crowd surrounded him. "Were you scared?" Philippine army chief of staff General Basilio Valdes asked him. "Yes sir," Villamor said, "I was very scared." Villamor "blessed the crater-pocked earth" where he stood. "It was hard to believe that I was still alive," he said.

CATHOLIC HOME FOR AGED LADIES (SITE)

This site (3043 P Street, NW) served as the Catholic Home for Aged Ladies for many years, beginning around 1913, when it moved from its original N Street location, until the mid-1950s, when it moved to another location. The home provided "residence for unsupported and elderly gentlewomen of Washington and its vicinities." Despite its name, it was nonsectarian; unusually, it was also kept "in the style and spirit of a private home."

In 1921, Joseph A. Mulry, SJ, said his first mass here shortly after his ordination in the Georgetown University chapel and following the completion of his philosophy and theology studies at Woodstock in Maryland. In 1924, he moved to the Philippines, where he served as a missionary for more than twenty years until his death in 1945. Mulry's work—both as a literature professor and as a pioneering advocate for social justice—was deeply consequential. He taught numerous students at the Ateneo, the Jesuit university in Manila, many of whom went on to play pivotal roles in public life. An annual literary award given by Ateneo is named after him.

One of his students was Horacio de la Costa SJ—the first Filipino provincial superior of the Philippine Jesuits and a distinguished Philippine historian—who called him "Prince of Teachers." ("He taught us the use of words," de la Costa recalled. "Words, he used to say, have a literal meaning, often pedestrian; but they also have overtones and undertones, which are magic.") Mulry organized a forum for reflecting on the church's social teachings and the most urgent social issues of that period: land reform and workers' rights. Mulry inspired Johnny Tan to convene the Federation of Free Workers, an organization of workers unions, and Jeremias Montemayor to launch the Federation of Free Farmers. "Because of that influence," Miguel Bernad, SJ, wrote, "he could be called the founder of the movement for social justice among Catholics in the Philippines."

In addition to inspiring social reformists, Mulry was much loved by his students. They called him "Father Pitong." Decades later, they still remembered his good humor, how he took their juvenile pranks in stride and made gentle fun of what they thought was fashionable, such as pomades (which he called "jaguar sweat").

In 1942, the Japanese put him in prison in Fort Santiago. He was kept in a small cell along with twenty to thirty other men, fed very little and made to sit all day, not allowed to talk to anyone. He was later released ("Mistake. Innocent. You go," they told him), but by then he was, according to his friend Vincent de Paul O'Beirne, SJ, "a broken man." He was brought to an internment camp in June 1944. At night, his friend James B. Reuter, SJ, said, "by the light of a burning wick floating in coconut oil in a corned beef can," Mulry talked about "Shakespeare, Keats, Robert Burns." "All the men who listened to him were hungry, but he fed us with beauty," Reuter said, "and it filled us better than food."

A few months later, just prior to the liberation of the Philippines, he suffered intense bleeding from stomach ulcers that he had first contracted at Fort Santiago. A surgeon later found that he had a "perforated ulcer of the stomach and incipient cancer." He was brought to an emergency facility but died within minutes. "You cannot imagine the sorrow and shock felt by all the priests and sisters at his sudden departure," O'Beirne wrote. Just moments before, Reuter had offered to carry Mulry from a bed to a stretcher. "Oh I don't need help!" Mulry said, as he slid himself onto the stretcher. "He was never any trouble," Reuter said. "Even when he was dying, he was never any trouble."

"Country is literally the land where you were born," Mulry told de la Costa, as they reflected on the meaning of words. "But if that is all, why do men die for their country?" In January 1945, Mulry died on an operating table in an internment camp, after serving tirelessly for more than twenty years in a country not his own.

JOHN F. KERRY AND TERESA HEINZ RESIDENCE

John F. Kerry is a decorated Vietnam War veteran who famously became an antiwar activist. In his long career in public service, he has served as U.S. senator and as secretary of state. He is also a Georgetown resident and, together with his wife, Teresa Heinz, owns a house on 33rd and O Streets.

Kerry has special ties to the Philippines. His grandfather's cousin William Cameron Forbes ("Cousin Cam") was governor general in the Philippines from 1909 to 1913 as President Theodore Roosevelt's appointee and later wrote a book on Philippine history, *The Philippine Islands*. Although Kerry struggled with the "paternalistic attitudes" toward the Philippines of the period that Forbes had helped articulate, Kerry recalls the "seemingly endless supply of beautiful mahogany wood baskets and cabinets, mottled, beeswing, and curly" that Forbes brought back from the Philippines. "We grew up with these exotic artifacts," Kerry wrote in his memoirs, "and I would say to myself, 'Wow, what an amazing place that must be. I want to go there someday.'"

And he did visit, twice, during one of the most critical periods of postwar Philippine history. In his autobiography, he described meeting Philippine president Ferdinand Marcos ("a brutal but reliable Cold War ally") soon after Kerry was first elected senator, as a member of a delegation to the Philippines led by Republican senator Richard Lugar. "After five hours alone with Ferdinand Marcos in the Malacañang Palace," Kerry wrote, "I was convinced that the United States need to change its policy towards the Philippines."

Following a disputed national election in early 1986, some thirty Philippine government employees—almost all of whom were women— walked out of a canvassing center, protesting what they said was systematic fraud to keep Marcos in power. "These are the most damning comments I've heard and the most dramatic incident I witnessed since I came," Kerry, who had traveled back to the Philippines as an election monitor, told the *Washington Post* then.

The government employees found refuge in a church. "One by one, the women stood by the altar, the klieg lights giving them the soft glow of a halo, and one by one they told the world that Marcos was cheating," Kerry recalled. "Their courage and the courage of the Filipino people lit a spark that traveled around the world," he said.

WOODLEY PARK

SHOREHAM HOTEL

While in exile during the war, Commonwealth president Manuel L. Quezon and his family stayed at the Shoreham Hotel, on the second floor of this large, sprawling building. Quezon's family had spent the summer of 1942 at Belmont (see "Metro D.C. Region" chapter) and moved to the Shoreham later in the year. "They have taken an apartment in one of the wings," the *Evening Star* announced in August, "and it is now in the process of being done over for them." The announcement added that the apartment included "a large living room, dining room, kitchen, and several bedrooms with a small porch overlooking the park." "To this day," his grandson Manolo Quezon recently wrote, "the only suite with a glassed-in balcony is that which was the residence of President Quezon in the Shoreham Hotel."

The suite also served as Quezon's office as he met regularly with members of the Commonwealth government, including Sergio Osmeña (vice-president), Andres Soriano (secretary of finance), Basilio Valdes (secretary of national defense), Jaime Hernandez (auditor-general), Carlos P. Romulo (secretary of information), Joaquín Elizalde (resident commissioner) and Arturo Rotor (executive secretary). The seventh anniversary of the Commonwealth later that year was celebrated at the Shoreham, with a radio broadcast of speeches by Quezon and President Franklin Roosevelt and live music performed by the soprano Enya Gonzalez accompanied on the piano by Rodolfo Cornejo (see "White House" chapter). "The heart of

Vintage postcard of the Shoreham Hotel, circa 1940. *Author's collection.*

the Philippine Government in Exile is a ten-room suite on the second floor of Washington's swank Shoreham Hotel," TIME magazine wrote.

But many of the photographs taken at the Shoreham during that period show Quezon visibly weak, in a reclining chair surrounded by Commonwealth officials. "In the sequestered stillness of his deep-carpeted rooms, Manuel Quezon moves quietly," TIME magazine said. He was a shadow of "the man of explosive talk and volatile gestures." Afflicted with tuberculosis for many years, the "damp underground shelters of Corregidor had so grievously racked his lungs," LIFE magazine wrote. Quezon, the magazine said, rarely moved. "Except for his eyes, he seems impassive," TIME magazine said.

Nonetheless, the work continued and Quezon met with Filipino and American officials when he could. Rotor, a writer and a medical doctor, wrote some years later, "By nature impulsive, his far-ranging mind rebelled at the restrictions imposed by his frail body." "Flat on his back, staring at the ceiling all day, deprived of the activities that gave his life a meaning, separated from his native land by a continent and an ocean," Rotor added, "President Quezon must have undergone the torments of hell."

The renowned labor activist and Filipino American writer Carlos Bulosan recalled meeting Quezon during this period, less than a year before Quezon died. Bulosan had a flourishing writing career, having just published an essay in the *Saturday Evening Post* alongside Norman Rockwell's iconic *Freedom from*

This page: The Omni Shoreham Hotel. *Photo by the author.*

Want painting of a Thanksgiving meal, part of Rockwell's Four Freedoms series. Bulosan wrote movingly of immigrant life. "If you want to know what we are, look upon the farms or upon the hard pavements of the city," Bulosan said.

At Quezon's request, Romulo asked Bulosan—who was in D.C. from the West Coast for a brief visit in November 1943 and was preparing to leave for New York—to meet Quezon at the Shoreham. Bulosan "rushed to his hotel trembling with fear," he wrote, anxious to meet the man who had de facto led the Philippines over Bulosan's lifetime ("the leader of the Filipino people for the last thirty-five years!" he said).

The Shoreham, Bulosan said, was a "vast building," and he spent an hour trying to find Quezon's secretary. Finally, he was led to Quezon's room. Quezon had difficulty speaking. "Now and then his hand went to his mouth as though he were urging the words to come out," Bulosan recalled. "I sat waiting for the words that did not come out, from a man who has said millions of words in his lifetime," Bulosan said.

But somehow, they managed to have a brief conversation about Quezon's extraordinary life and how Bulosan thought it needed to be written, as "the story of his life is the actual history of the Philippines."

"Would you like to do it?" Quezon asked. Bulosan was taken by surprise and was unable to say anything. "I felt that I was incapable of writing the life story of so great a man," he later recalled. Bulosan sat quietly for a few more minutes until he was "prodded by [Quezon's] secretary to accept it."

But Quezon was in pain again, and the visit was cut short. They shook hands, and Bulosan left, overwhelmed. It was the last time he saw Quezon. Three years later Bulosan published *America is in the Heart*, his landmark novel. He died in the mid-1950s without ever writing the book he had reluctantly agreed to write.

DE VEYRA RESIDENCE

The de Veyra family lived here (2610 Cathedral Avenue) while Jaime C. de Veyra served as Philippine resident commissioner, a nonvoting member of U.S. Congress. Their grandchildren have preserved a 1919 group photograph taken on the front yard of this residence, and the address appears in directories from that period.

Ellen Slayden, the wife of Texas congressman James L. Slayden, remembers meeting Sofia over dinner a few months after their arrival in Washington. In

The former residence of suffrage leader Sofia de Veyra at 2610 Cathedral Avenue, 1917. *Courtesy of Binggay Montilla.*

her diary, published posthumously, she admitted her apprehension prior to their meeting, noting that it was "her first excursion from the islands." "I had rather dreaded meeting her," she wrote.

Sofia turned out to be astonishing. "She was prettily dressed," Ellen wrote, "and her English was impeccable, and she talked with knowledge and vivacity on politics, especially, as well as books, Spanish and English, religion, the woman's movement and domestic science." Sofia had experienced racial bias but showed "a keen and humorous sense of the prejudice she met here." "She was not resentful," Ellen said, "but evidently means to safeguard her dignity." Ellen thought Sofia would have been "graceful" company anywhere. "Mrs. De Veyra opened my provincial eyes," she recalled.

When Sofia first moved to Washington, she was already extraordinarily accomplished, despite receiving only a few years of formal education. She helped set up the first Philippine nursing school. She was the founding officer of a women's organization, *Asociacion Feminista Filipina*, and founding officer of an organization that promoted maternal and child health, *Gota de Leche*, now among the oldest Philippine nongovernment organizations. She had also taught English and had served as dormitory dean of an academic institute.

The former residence of suffrage leader Sofia de Veyra at 2610 Cathedral Avenue. *Photo by the author.*

In Washington, Sofia was just as tireless. In addition to her responsibilities as mother to four children and duties as Jaime's de facto secretary (Ellen said Jaime "spoke little English"), she immediately volunteered her time at a local congressional Red Cross Unit and Community Center Unit, contributing numerous hours of work knitting sweaters and socks for U.S. soldiers and making hospital clothes. "She was one of the few in the

District of Columbia to be awarded the Red Cross medal for having done more than eight hundred hours' work," Frank Pyle wrote for the *Women's Home Journal*, "as well as to be given the certificate signed by the President in acknowledgement of articles made."

Sofia traveled around the country to educate Americans about Philippine life. She famously gave "illustrated lectures" using stereo cards and Philippine souvenirs (see "Foggy Bottom" chapter) and once put together a "made-in-the-Philippines" banquet in Missouri, featuring Philippine dishes accompanied by Philippine music, furniture and crafts. She was a leader of the Philippine suffrage movement, led a delegation of Philippine women to meet with Mrs. Harding (see "White House and Neighborhood" chapter) and joined the Pan Am Conference of Women in Baltimore. Her pronouncements on the status of Philippine women were quoted widely. "The women over there [the Philippines] can do most everything a man can do," she told the *Washington Post*. Sofia de Veyra was a "live wire," according to the *Midland Journal*, "the best known Filipina in America."

The de Veyra family first arrived in Washington in 1917 and stayed until the end of Jaime's term in 1923. Although Jaime was officially his country's representative, it was his wife, Sofia, who tangibly changed the way many Americans came to view the Philippines. "Those who have doubts about the ability of the Filipinos to govern themselves should have heard the illustrated lecture by Mme. de Veyra in the Public Library yesterday afternoon on 'Yesterday and Today in the Philippines,'" the *Boston Globe* wrote, "and they would have most of their doubts dissipated."

MANUEL VIRAY RESIDENCE

Manuel Viray, Philippine foreign service officer and writer, lived here (2150 Cathedral Avenue, NW) in the 1960s while serving in the Philippine embassy. He and his family moved to D.C. beginning in the mid-1950s, as he took on the first of several overseas assignments. His diplomatic posts included Cambodia in 1975, where, along with a handful of embassy staff, he stayed on until just before Phnom Penh fell to the Khmer Rouge and then boarded the last Air Cambodia flight out of the capital, but only after ensuring the evacuation of all Filipino nationals. "Viray probably saved thousands of his people," Michael Semel wrote for the *Norfolk Compass/Virginian-Pilot*.

In addition to his diplomatic career, Viray was an accomplished writer. ("Diplomacy is not only a form of words, but a form of treachery," he once

The former residence of Manuel Viray at 2150 Cathedral Avenue. *Photo by the author.*

said.) He was a member of a prewar group of Filipino writers called The Veronicans ("it was their aim to make their writing bear the imprint of the face of the Philippines, just as the cloth of Veronica bore imprint of Christ," according to Herbert Schneider, SJ) and published several books, including anthologies of Philippine poetry as well as those of his own. His literary correspondence with writer and fellow D.C. resident Bienvenido N. Santos is preserved in L.M. Grow's *The Epistolary Criticism of Manuel A. Viray: In Memoriam* (1998). They were both among the first Filipino writers in English.

About half the poems in Viray's collection *After This Exile* (1965) are on his life in D.C. He wrote movingly about places around the city and the city's ever-changing seasons, including a poem about Rock Creek Park ("Speckled, speckling the bleakness of wintry trees, / Dividing my three girls' excited babble") and his home on Cathedral Avenue ("Here the seasons mingle / In the shut and rancid air"). Poet Richard Eberhart said, "[Viray's] poems express a teeming sense of the world. He is aware of the dance of sense and feel's the dance of sensory meaning against a backdrop of man's limitations, his ultimate destruction." His poems, Eberhart wrote, are "nervously alive."

Viray lived in near obscurity in Virginia toward the end of his life, having left the Philippines during the Marcos period—"to escape possible imprisonment," he told Semel, as he had been publicly critical of Marcos. He lived in a modest retirement home away from family in Norfolk, although had trouble making payments, having lost access to his pension. ("Because he lost track of his daughter, who was receiving Viray's pension check, Viray hasn't been able to pay the whole $550 room and board at the home," Semel wrote.) A local church provided financial support, and he did part-time menial work in exchange ("taking out the garbage and locking up at night"). "Once a hero, now lives in humility," Semel wrote. "I have a residue of anger," he told Semel, "But *c'est la vie*." Viray died soon after he turned eighty in 1997.

Around 1960, he sat with Santos on the porch of his Cathedral Avenue home—"one sweltering, humid summer, swinging on the glider"—and talked about poetry. "Have you ever noticed that the weather, the seasons, penetrate, bounce off, glitter, and affect the skin and acts of the people, the figures in my poems?" he asked. "That's what I was going to tell you in a minute," Santos said.

METRO D.C. REGION

*I*n a country that has shaped much of world history in the twentieth century and in a capital city of monuments and museums, one inevitably finds references to the Philippines all over the city and the metro region. The Navy Memorial on Pennsylvania Avenue, for example, honors the men and women who served with the U.S. Navy, including those who served with the Asiatic Fleet in the Philippines. At the World War II Memorial, a pillar lists the Philippines among U.S. territories during the period. The Southern Fountains name major battles of the war, including references to Bataan, Corregidor and Leyte, among others. The Marine Corps Memorial (also known as the Iwo Jima Memorial) in Rosslyn, Virginia, stands just across the river from Georgetown, "in honor and memory of the men of the United States Marine Corps," as the inscription states, "who have given their lives to their country since November 1775." Around the base of the monument are the many wars in which the marines served, including what it calls the "Philippine insurrection" and the Second World War, notably in Bataan and Corregidor.

ARLINGTON CEMETERY

Countless soldiers who served in the Spanish-American War, the Philippine-American War and the Second World War are buried in Arlington Cemetery, including Filipino soldiers who served with U.S. Army Forces in the Far East. Close to the Tomb of the Unknown Solider is the USS *Maine* Mast Memorial,

Manuel Quezon's funeral procession, Arlington Cemetery, August 1944. *Courtesy of the Quezon Family Collection.*

inaugurated by President Woodrow Wilson in 1915 in honor of those who died in the mysterious 1898 explosion of the USS *Maine*, which then led to the Spanish-American War and eventually the Philippine-American War. The memorial features the original mast of the USS *Maine* and the *Maine*'s bell, fused on to the door of the memorial's base.

When Commonwealth president Manuel L. Quezon died while in exile on August 1, 1944, his remains were kept at the base of this memorial until after the end of the war, when they were transferred to Manila. It is a curious footnote to Philippine history: Quezon's public life began during the Philippine-American War, fighting alongside General Emilio Aguinaldo. At Cabanatuan, he served as Aguinaldo's staff, as Quezon wrote in his posthumously published autobiography, *The Good Fight*. (He saw Aguinaldo shortly after Aguinaldo was captured by the Americans. "I am…very well treated by the Americans, but a prisoner just the same," the general told him.) In 1944, nearly half a century after the sinking of the USS *Maine*, a Philippine president who had fought for independence his entire life was buried at this memorial.

FRONT ROYAL, VIRGINIA

Captain Parker Hitt joined the U.S. Army during the Spanish-American War and served in the Philippines during the Philippine-American War. He later became a colonel and a pioneer military cryptographer, along with his wife, Genevieve Young Hitt, who, according to his biographer, Betsy Rohaly Smoot, might have been the first woman to serve as a military cryptographer. Colonel Hitt's manual on military cryptography, *Manual for the Solution of Military Ciphers*, was an important reference in the First World War and was reprinted and continued to be in use during the Second World War. He died on March 2, 1971, in Front Royal, Virginia, at the age of ninety-three.

At a used books store in Winchester, Virginia, not too far from Front Royal a few years ago, my family and I found a book previously owned by Colonel Hitt. It was a gift from his father according to an inscription on the first page ("Presented to Captain Parker Hitt, U.S. Army, by his father. January, 1912"). The last page of the book contained Colonel Hitt's handwritten notes on General Emilio Aguinaldo's cipher letters, their current location among the Philippine Insurgent Records and the cipher to decrypt them. We donated the book to the National Cryptologic Museum in Annapolis, and we hope it is of use to historians and researchers.

WALTER REED HOSPITAL

Major Peyton March famously led U.S. troops at the Battle of Tirad Pass against Filipino soldiers led by General Gregorio del Pilar (see also "White House and Neighborhood" chapter). "Our losses were 2 killed 9 wounded," it says in his diary. "The enemy left 8 dead upon the road," he wrote, "among whom was Gregorio del Pilar." Del Pilar's remains were treated disgracefully by March's men. "The rest of the Filipinos routed, the U.S. soldiers flew out like buzzards to strip del Pilar's body of everything from his pants and collar button to a locket containing a curl of woman's hair and an American twenty-dollar gold piece he had carried in his pocket," Stanley Karnow wrote. "The cadaver lay naked in the sun for days."

Del Pilar, the "Boy General," was only twenty-four; March was thirty-three and would live a very long life. At the height of his distinguished military career, he served as U.S. Army chief of staff and presided over the mobilization of more than 1 million American soldiers for the First World

Walter Reed Army Hospital, circa 2011. *Carol M. Highsmith Archive, Library of Congress, Prints and Photographs Division.*

War and their demobilization after. "He was," General Douglas MacArthur once said, "perhaps the greatest Chief of Staff of all time."

His son, Peyton March Jr., died from an aviation accident in 1918, about a year after joining the U.S. Army Air Corps. He was only twenty-one. President Theodore Roosevelt, whose own son Quentin served in the same army branch and was killed in action not long after, wrote to March, "I thank you, Sir. You have already drunk of the waters of bitterness; I suppose I shall soon have to drink of them; but whatever befalls, you and I hold our heads high when we think of our sons."

On February 3, 1954, soon after turning eighty-nine, March broke a hip and spent the next fourteen months at the Walter Reed Hospital until his death in April 1955. He stayed in one of the upper rooms with a view of the garden. As his eyesight deteriorated, hospital staff gave him an electric clock "with especially large hands."

FAIRFAX, VIRGINIA

Francis Burton Harrison served as governor general of the Philippines from 1913 to 1921, and as mentioned in previous chapters, he implemented the swift integration of Filipino officials into government administration, as the number of Filipino officials increased twofold, while the number of American officials fell by more than two-thirds, during his term. Harrison was a descendant of Reverend Bryan Fairfax, the cousin of Thomas Fairfax, the Sixth Lord Fairfax of Cameron, after whom Fairfax, Virginia, is named. His father served as secretary to Jefferson Davis, the Confederate president.

Years after serving as governor general, Harrison returned to the Philippines to serve as adviser to the newly formed Commonwealth government. A September 1936 entry in his diary describes a meeting between his young son "Kiko" and President Quezon. "Kiko, having born here, could upon reaching the age of 21, choose whether he wished to be an American or a Philippine citizen," Harrison wrote, "in which respect he had a wider choice than myself." At Quezon's recommendation one month later, the National Assembly granted Philippine citizenship to Harrison. "It is not necessary for me to state that no American has contributed more to the cause of Philippine self-government and independence than the Honorable Francis Burton Harrison and that he deserves the eternal gratitude of our people," Quezon said. Harrison spent many more years serving the Philippine government in both formal and informal capacities, including during the war.

Harrison died in 1957 and, following instructions in his last will, is buried in the Philippines. He was a Fairfax descendant, the son of a Confederate staff member, an American public servant and a Filipino citizen, by choice.

BELMONT COUNTRY CLUB

Quezon and his family stayed at the Belmont Country Club in the summer of 1942 before moving to their new quarters at the Shoreham Hotel (see "Woodley Park" chapter). Belmont is also known as the Hurley Estate after its owner, Patrick Hurley, who served as secretary of war and U.S. minister to New Zealand. The mansion is in Ashburn, Virginia, though identified as Leesburg, Virginia, in some Commonwealth documents. "The President and Mrs. Quezon, having leased Belmont for a year, will continue to spend their weekends there even after they take over the suite at the Shoreham," the *Evening Star* announced in August 1942. ("At 5:30 p.m. left with President Quezon

The Quezon family at the Belmont Country Club. *Courtesy of the Quezon Family Collection.*

for Belmont Plantation Leesburg," General Basilio Valdes, the secretary of national defense, wrote in his diary the following month.)

A famous group photograph was taken at Belmont in June 1942 of the Quezon family, members of the Commonwealth cabinet and their friends. Reproduced widely, the photograph is an extraordinary gathering of some of the most important figures in Philippines history, in addition to Quezon himself: Vice-President Sergio Osmeña, who succeeded Quezon as commonwealth president; Carlos P. Romulo, who became a world leader and the country's principal diplomat; Estefania Aldaba Lim, who became founding president of the nation's first children's museum, among her many accomplishments in a long distinguished career in public service; General Basilio Valdes, secretary of defense who had an illustrious career in both medicine and military service; and others who would someday soon help rebuild the Philippines and become leaders of a sovereign republic. In the photograph, too, are a few individuals who stayed on past the war, raised families and lived private lives in the metro D.C. region.

Belmont Country Club in Ashburn, Virginia. *Photo by the author.*

The Commonwealth Government in Exile at the Belmont Country Club, Ashburn, Virginia, 1942. The Quezon family are in the front row. *Courtesy of Ricardo Lim and the Quezon Family Collection.*

Much like the rest of this volume, the Belmont photograph captures remarkable individuals who found temporary and permanent homes in their adopted city, a moment in time in the midst of the chaos and turbulence of the twentieth century, a still point in the lives of people in the entwined destinies of the United States and the Philippines.

BIBLIOGRAPHY

Published Secondary Sources

Agoncillo, Teodoro A., and Milagros C. Guerrero. *History of the Filipino People*. Quezon City, PH: Malaya Books, 1969.

Alcazaren, Paulo. "Building a City Beautiful." *Philippine Star*, July 5, 2003.

Arroyo, Nenette. "First Lady Helen Taft's Luneta Remembered in Washington's Potomac Park." *White House History Quarterly*, no. 34 (2013): 54–69.

Bradford, James C. *Quarterdeck and Bridge: Two Centuries of American Naval Leaders*. Annapolis, MD: Naval Institute Press, 2013.

Brown, Kellie D. *The Sound of Hope: Music as Solace, Resistance and Salvation during the Holocaust and World War II*. Jefferson, NC: McFarland, 2020.

Buckley, Christopher. *Washington Schlepped Here: Walking in the Nation's Capital*. New York: Crown Journeys, 2003.

Bueza, Michael. "Fast Facts: Helena Zoila Benitez Is 100 Years old." *Rappler*, June 27, 2014.

Cacas, Rita, and Juanita Tamayo Lott. *Filipinos in Washington, D.C.* Charleston, SC: Arcadia Publishing, 2009.

Carandang, Teresa, and Erwin R. Tiongson. "Finding Philippine Art in Washington DC." *Asian Journal* (March 2014). Reprinted in *Philippine Philatelic Journal* 36, no. 2 (Second Quarter 2014): 34–35.

———. "Florence Harding Welcomes Philippine Women to the White House: Suffragist Leaders Identified in White House Photograph." *White House Historical Quarterly*, no 53 (Spring 2019): 74–83.

————. "In the Footsteps of Philippine Presidents." *Vault Magazine* 5, no.4 (January 2015): 75–87.

Carandang, Teresa, Ginger Potenciano and Erwin R. Tiongson. "Frederic Ossorio: Monuments Man." *Metro Home & Entertaining Magazine* 13, no. 2 (2016): 44.

Carandang, Teresa. "A D.C. Springtime Concert Born in Manila." *Positively Filipino*, April 24, 2013.

————. "Galo's Road: The Journeys of an Arlington Resident." *Arlington Connection*, July 11–17, 2018.

————. "The Manila House in Washington, DC." *Positively Filipino*, May 10, 2017.

————. "The Quezons at the White House." *Positively Filipino*, June 7, 2018.

————. "The Thoroughly Modern Sofia de Veyra," *Positively Filipino*, August 7, 2013.

Churchill, Bernardita Reyes. *The Philippine Independence Missions to the United States, 1919–1934*. Manila, PH: National Historical Institute, 1983.

Coffman, Edward M. *The Hilt of the Sword: The Career of Peyton C. March*. Madison: University of Wisconsin Press, 1966.

Coit, Margaret L. *Mr. Baruch*. Washington, D.C.: Beard Books, 2000.

Cordery, Stacy A. *Alice: Alice Roosevelt Longworth, from White House Princess to Washington Power Broker*. New York: Viking, 2007.

Cummins, Paul F. *Dachau Song: The Twentieth-Century Odyssey of Herbert Zipper*. New York: Peter Lang Publishing, 1992.

Cunningham, Roger D. "The Loving Touch." *Army History* (Summer 2007): 5–25.

DeFerrari, John. *Historic Restaurants of Washington, D.C.: Capital Eats*. Charleston, SC: The History Press, 2013.

De Ocampo, Esteban. *First Filipino Diplomat*. Manila, PH: National Historical Institute, 1978.

Doeppers, Daniel F. "Manila's Imperial Makeover: Security, Health, and Symbolism." In *Colonial Crucible*. Edited by Alfred W. McCoy and Francisco A. Scarano. Madison: University of Wisconsin Press, 2009.

Federman, Adam. *Fasting and Feasting: The Life of Visionary Food Writer Patience Gray*. London: White River Junction, 2017.

Fermin, Jose D. 1904 *World's Fair: The Filipino Experience*. West Conshohocken, PA: Infinity Publishing, 2004.

Gould, Lewis L. *Helen Taft: Our Musical First Lady*. Lawrence: University Press of Kansas, 2010.

————. *My Dearest Nellie: The Letters of William Howard Taft to Helen Herron Taft, 1909–1912*. Lawrence: University Press of Kansas, 2011.

Grant, James. *Bernard M. Baruch: The Adventures of a Wall Street Legend*. New York: J. Wiley, 2012.

Grow, L.M. *The Epistolary Criticism of Manuel A. Viray: In Memoriam*. Quezon City, PH: Giraffe Books, 1998.

Guillermo, Alice. *The Life and Times of Galo B. Ocampo*. Manila, PH: McEnrho Book Publishing, 2013.

Halstead, Murat. *The Life and Achievements of Admiral Dewey: From Montpelier to Manila*. Chicago: Our Possessions Publishing Company, 1899.

Hess, Stephen. *Bit Player: My Life with Presidents and Ideas*. Washington, D.C.: Brookings Institution Press, 2018.

Hines Thomas S. "The Imperial Façade: Daniel H. Burnham and American Architectural Planning in the Philippines." *Pacific Historical Review* 41, no. 1 (February 1972): 33–53.

Immerwahr, Daniel. *How to Hide an Empire: A History of the Greater United States*. New York: Picador, 2019.

Karnow, Stanley. *In Our Image: America's Empire in the Philippines*. New York: Random House, 1989.

Lee, Karis. "A Filipino Literary Landmark: The Manila House in D.C." Boundary Stones, WETA's Local History Website, January 30, 2020. https://boundarystones.weta.org/2020/01/30/filipino-literary-landmark-manila-house-dc.

Mojares, Resil. "The Formation of Filipino Nationality Under U.S. Colonial Rule." *Philippine Quarterly of Culture and Society* 34, no. 1 (March 2006): 11–32.

Montgomery, Ben. *The Leper Spy: The Story of an Unlikely Hero of World War II*. Chicago: Chicago Review Press, 2016.

Morley, Ian. *American Colonisation and the City Beautiful Filipinos and Planning in the Philippines, 1916–35*. London: Routledge, 2019.

Ocampo, Ambeth. "Bulilit na Kafamfangan." *Philippine Daily Inquirer*, May 27, 2022.

———. "A Stroll through Wilson House." *Philippine Daily Inquirer*, August 28, 2000.

Pacis, Vicente Albano. *President Sergio Osmeña: A Fully-Documented Biography*. Manila: Philippine Constitution Association, 1971.

Paras-Perez, Rodolfo. *Tolentino*. Malolos, Bulacan: National Art Foundation of Malolos, 1976.

Pasachoff, Naomi E. *Alexander Graham Bell: Making Connections*. New York: Oxford University Press, 1996.

Pilar, Santiago Albano Pilar. *Pamana: The Jorge B. Vargas Art Collection*. Quezon City, PH: Committee on Arts and Culture, Vargas Centennial Celebrations, U.P. Vargas Museum, 1992.

Quirino, Carlos. "The First Philippine Imprints." *Journal of History* 8, no. 3 (1960): 219–28.

Richardson, Claiborne T. "The Filipino-American Phenomenon: The Loving Touch." *Black Perspective in Music* 10, no. 1 (Spring 1982): 3–28.

Romulo, Liana. "When Lolo's Debating Team Vanquished America." *Positively Filipino,* July 3, 2013.

Rozek, Stacy A. "The First Daughter of the Land: Alice Roosevelt as Presidential Celebrity, 1902–1906." *Presidential Studies Quarterly* 19, no. 1 (Winter 1989): 51–70.

Salina Journal. "Ike Yearned to Fly but Landed in Politics." December 25, 1994, 3.

Scharnhorst, Gary. *The Life of Mark Twain: The Final Years, 1891–1910.* Columbia: University of Missouri Press, 2022.

Schneider, Herbert, SJ. "The Period of Emergence of Philippine Letters (1930–1944)." In *Brown Heritage: Essays on Philippine Cultural Tradition and Literature.* Edited by Antonio G. Manuud. Quezon City, PH: Ateneo de Manila University, 1967.

Smoot, Betsy. *Rohaly Parker Hitt: The Father of American Military Cryptology.* Lexington: University Press of Kentucky, 2022.

Sta. Maria, Felice. *The Governor-General's Kitchen: Philippine Culinary Vignettes and Period Recipes, 1521–1935.* Pasig: Anvil, 2006.

Talusan, Mary. *Instruments of Empire: Filipino Musicians, Black Soldiers, and Military Band Music during the U.S. Colonization of the Philippines.* Jackson: University Press of Mississippi, 2021.

Tiongson, Erwin R. "Ike Learns to Fly." *Air & Space Museum Magazine* (September 2021): 107.

———. "Remembering an American Who Became Filipino 80 Years Ago." *Philippine Philatelic Journal* 39, no. 1 (First Quarter 2017): 39.

Tiongson, Ruel Hector R. "A Brush with Greatness." *Positively Filipino,* October 2, 2013.

Torres, May Arlene. "Interview with Isagani Giron." In *Goyo: Ang Batang Heneral: The History Behind the Movie.* Mandaluyong City, PH: Anvil Publishing, 2018.

Tuason, Julie A. "The Ideology of Empire in National Geographic Magazine's Coverage of the Philippines, 1898–1908." *Geographical Review* 89, No. 1 (January 1999): 34–53.

Urbina, Ian. "The Empire Strikes Back." *Village Voice,* January 28, 2003.

Valencia, Elpidio I. *President Sergio Osmeña.* Manila, PH: Dr. Elpidio I. Valencia, 1977.

Valeros, Florentino B., and Estrellita V. Gruenberg. *Filipino Writers in English*. Quezon City, PH: New Day, 1987.

Waldrup, Carole Chandler. *Wives of the American Presidents*. Jefferson, NC: McFarland & Company Inc., 2006.

Wolf, Edwin. *Doctrina Christiana: The First Book Printed in the Philippines, Manila, 1593*. A facsimile of the copy in the Lessing J. Rosenwald Collection, Library of Congress. Washington, D.C.: Library of Congress, 1947.

Yoder, Robert L. *In Performance: Walter Howard Loving and the Philippine Constabulary Band*. Manila, PH: National Historical Commission of the Philippines, 2013.

Published Primary Sources

Agoncillo, Marcella M. *Reminiscences of the Agoncillo Family*. Manila, PH: Felipe Agoncillo and Marcela Mariño de Agoncillo Foundation, 1981.

Albuquerque Citizen. "Mrs. Taft Wins Plaudits of Society." May 18, 1909, 3.

Alegre, Edilberto N., and Doreen Fernandez. *Writers and Their Milieu: An Oral History of Second-Generation Writers in English*. Manila, PH: De La Salle University Press, 1987.

American Architect. "Peace Statue for President Wilson." September 17, 1919, 383.

Aquino, Corazon. Speech before the Joint Session of the U.S. Congress, September 18, 1986. https://awpc.cattcenter.iastate.edu/2017/03/21/speech-before-the-joint-session-of-the-united-states-congress-sept-18-1986.

Bernad, Miguel A., SJ. *The Lights of Broadway and Other Essays*. Quezon City, PH: New Day Publishers, 1980.

———. "The Terrible Cost of Freedom." *Philippine Daily Inquirer*, October 8, 2007.

———. *Unusual and Ordinary: Biographical Sketches of Some Philippine Jesuits*. Quezon City, PH: Jesuit Communications Foundations Inc., 2006.

Borras, Peter. "Cabalistic Cookery." Letter. *Time* 24, no. 22 (November 26, 1934).

Boston Globe. "Irineo Esperancilla." July 15, 1938, 9.

———. "MME de Veyra Shows Filipino Progress." January 10, 1921, 4.

Buencamino, Felipe. *Memoirs and Diaries of Felipe Buencamino III, 1941–1944*. Makati City, PH: CopyCat, 2003.

Bulosan, Carlos. "Freedom from Want." *Saturday Evening Post*, March 6, 1943, 12.

————. "Manuel L. Quezon: The Good Fight." *Bataan* 11, no. 5 (1944): 13–15.

————. *Sound of Falling Light: Letters in Exile.* Edited by Dolores Feria. Quezon City, PH: Dolores Feria, 1960.

Burnham, Daniel H., and Edward H. Bennett. *Plan of Chicago.* Chicago: Commercial Club, Chicago, 1909.

Cronkhite, Russell. "The Prime Minister Wants Sugar Pops: And Other Secrets of a Blair House Chef." *Washington Post*, April 4, 2001, F1.

Daily Gateway. "Would Marry Alice Roosevelt: Sultan of Sulu Visits Taft Party and Is Smitten with President's Daughter." August 21, 1905, 1.

De la Costa, Horacio. "Joseph Mulry SJ." *Jesuit/Philippine Province* 20, no. 1 (March 1971): 15–18.

Douglass, Elmer. "Light Arias and Talkers Occupy Air." *Chicago Tribune*, May 17, 1924, 8.

Elsen, William A. "Gonzaga Building Plan Told: Gonzaga Plans to Build." *Washington Post*, March 11, 1973, D1.

Ephraim, Frank. *Escape to Manila: From Nazi Tyranny to Japanese Terror.* Champaign: University of Illinois Press, 2003.

Evening Star. "Filipinos Depart." June 13, 1904, 6.

————. "Group of Filipinos Ask Independence." January 3, 1930, B5.

————. "Mrs. Roosevelt Gives Fete for Senora de Somoza." August 25, 1942, B3.

————. "Police Raid Social Club, 53 Poker Players Arrested." February 21, 1951, A5.

————. "Quezon Gets Ovation in House; Says Filipinos Will Fight On." June 2, 1942, 1.

————. "Quezon Takes 6-Month Lease on Belmont, Virginia Estate." June 5, 1942, A16.

————. "Taft's Own' Filipino Band." March 5, 1909, 13.

————. "Taps Sounded Over Heroes of Maine." March 24, 1912, 1.

————. "Tribute of Nation to Martyred Sons." March 23, 1912, 11.

————. "Turns Back on Manila." June 28, 1922, 12.

Gallagher, Patrick. "Quezon's Farewell to Congress that Becomes Congress' Farewell to Quezon." *Philippine Review* 1, no. 10 (October 1916): 11–20.

Hailey, Albon B. "Free World Mourns Death of Magsaysay." *Washington Post* and *Times Herald*, March 18, 1957, B2.

Harrison, Francis Burton. *The Corner-Stone of Philippine Independence: A Narrative of Seven Years.* New York: Century Company, 1922.

————. *Origins of the Philippine Republic: Extracts from the Diaries and Records of Francis Burton Harrison.* New York: Cornell University, 1974.

Honolulu Star-Bulletin. "Constabulary Band Due Here in Manchuria." February 3, 1915, 4.

Hurley, John F., SJ. *Wartime Superior in the Philippines*. Quezon City, PH: Ateneo de Manila University Press, 2005.

Kansas City Star. "Music and Musicians." July 13, 1924, 5D.

Kerry, John F. *Every Day Is Extra*. New York: Simon & Schuster, 2018.

Kraus, Hans Peter. *A Rare Book Saga: The Autobiography of H. P. Kraus*. New York: G.P. Putnam's Sons, 1978.

Library of Congress. "Library of Congress Footnotes." *Information Bulletin* 18, no. 2, (January 12, 1959): 22–24.

LIFE. "The Great Filipino" (November 15, 1943): 36–37.

Longworth, Alice Roosevelt. *Crowded Hours: Reminisces of Alice Roosevelt Longworth*. New York: C. Scribner's Sons, 1933.

Lyons, Leonard. "Loose-Leaf Notebook." *Washington Post*, August 24, n.d., 9.

Macapagal, Diosdado. *A Stone for the Edifice: Memoirs of a President*. Manila, PH: Mac Publishing House, 1968.

March, Peyton C. *The Nation at War*. Garden City, NJ: Doubleday, Doran & Company, 1932.

McNair, Marie. "Stalwarts See Philippine Battles Become Streets." *Washington Post*, April 10, 1961, B4.

Mellon, Paul. *Reflections in a Silver Spoon: A Memoir*. New York: William Morrow and Company, 1992.

Midland Journal. "Meet the De Veyra Family." August 27, 1920, 5.

National Gallery of Art Annual Report. Washington, D.C.: National Gallery of Art, 1974.

National Gallery of Art Annual Report. Washington, D.C.: National Gallery of Art, 1973.

New York Times. "Ton of Ice Cools Cabinet: Members, Hot in Own Room, Adjourn to President Taft's Office." July 8, 1911, 3.

———. "W. Morgan Shuster Dead at 83; Led Appleton-Century-Crofts." May 27, 1960, 31.

———. "Wide to Ride with Taft: Will Accompany Him Back from Capitol—Supreme Court Bible Chosen." March 1, 1909, 1.

Omang, Joanne. "Aquino Appeals to Congress: Philippine Leader's Emotional Speech Wins Votes for Aid." *Washington Post*, September 19, 1986, A1.

Parks, Lillian Rogers. *My Thirty Years Backstairs at the White House*. New York: Fleet Publishing Corporation, 1961.

Pershing, John. *My Life Before the World War, 1860–1917: A Memoir*. Lexington: University of Kentucky Press, 2013.

Philippine Republic. "Mrs. Recto Pleases Washington Society." October 1924, 11.

———. "Santiago's Triumph Is the Real Thing." October 1924, 10.

Preston, Peggy. "No Rustic Bard Is Jose Villa." *Washington Post*, September 15, 1942, B7.

Quezon, Manuel Luis. *The Good Fight*. New York: D. Appleton-Century Company, 1946.

Rainey, Ada. "Art World's Plans Aided by Congress." *Washington Post*, December 26, 1926, F2.

Reuter, James B., SJ. "With the Rains Come Memories." In *Mission to Mankind*. New York: Random House, 1963.

Richmond Palladium. "Audience Arose When National Air Was Played." February 27, 1909, 1.

Romulo, Carlos P. "Bataan's Meaning—19 Years Later." *Washington Post*, April 9, 1961, E4.

———. *I Walked with Heroes*. New York: Holt, Rinehart, and Winston, 1961.

———. *My Brother Americans*. New York: Doubleday, Doran, and Company, 1945.

Romulo, Carlos P., and Beth Day Romulo. *The Philippine Presidents: Memoirs of Carlos P. Romulo*. Quezon City, PH: New Day, 1988.

Rotor, Arturo B., MD. *Confidentially, Doctor*. Quezon City, PH: Phoenix Publishing House, 1965.

Santos, Bienvenido. *Memory's Fiction: A Personal History*. Quezon City, PH: New Day, 1993.

Semel, Michael. "Storied Past: Filipino, Once a Hero, Now Lives in Humility." *Norfolk Compass* and *Virginian-Pilot*, January 15, 1989, 1, 8–9.

Sherrod, Robert. "Toughest Guy in the Air Force." *Saturday Evening Post*, March 26, 1955, 144.

Shuster, W. Morgan. "Our Philippine Policies and Their Results." *Journal of Race Development* 1, no. 1 (July 1910): 58–74.

———. *The Strangling of Persia*. New York: Century Company, 1912.

Slayden, Ellen. *Washington Wife: Journal of Ellen Maury Slayden from 1897–1919*. New York: Harper & Row, 1963.

St. Louis-Globe Democrat. "Zup!" July 14, 1938, 24.

Taft, Helen Herron. *Recollections of Full Years*. New York: Dodd, Mead, 1914.

Taft, William Howard. "Facsimile of President Taft's Telegram on the Death of Mr. Burnham." In *Daniel H. Burnham: Architect Planner of Cities*. New York: Houghton Mifflin, 1921.

TIME. "Heroes" (July 9, 1948): 25–26.

————. "Problem in Exile" (November 1, 1943): 13.

University Hatchet. "Award Cites Jose Santos." October 21, 1958, 3.

U.S. Department of State. The President's Log at Tehran, November 27–December 2, 1943. U.S. Department of State. Foreign Relations of the United States Diplomatic Papers. The Conferences at Cairo and Tehran, 1943. Washington, D.C.: U.S. Department of State, 1943.

Villamor, Jesús A. *They Never Surrendered: A True Story of Resistance in World War II.* Quezon City, PH: Vera-Reyes, 1982.

Viray, Manuel. *After This Exile.* Quezon City, PH: Phoenix, 1965.

Washington Herald. "Filipino Band Farewell Concert." May 2, 1909, 5.

————. "Filipinos Pay Honor to Jose Rizal, Hero." December 31, 1913, 3.

Washington Post. "Art World Plans Aided by Congress." December 26, 1926, F2.

————. "Back from the Orient: Miss Roosevelt and Others on Their Way Here." October 24, 1905, 2.

————. "Bal Boheme Plans Made as Mystery." January 9, 1927: F5.

————. "Bond with the Philippines." April 9, 1961, E4.

————. "Col. Jesus Villamor." October 29, 1971, C6.

————. "Fahnsworth and His Wife Have Exhibit." January 16, 1927, F5.

————. "Filipinos in the City." June 10, 1904, 2.

————. "High Dignitaries of State to Attend Quezon Rites Today." August 5, 1944, 2.

————. "Irineo Esperancilla, 69, Steward for 4 Presidents." July 27, 1976, C4.

————. "Japan Spurs Islands." January 10, 1915, 4.

————. "Keen Eye on Filipinos." February 1, 1899, 9.

————. "Madrillon Food Feature as Cafe Marks 16 Years: Host Peter Borras Insists on Highest Standard; Spot Has History." April 8, 1936, 11.

————. "Magsaysay Mourners Fill St. Matthew's." March 24, 1957, B2.

————. "Mr. Forbes Is Honored By Prominent Filipinos." April 20, 1932, 8.

————. "Obituary: Joey Guerrero Leaumax, Kennedy Center Usher." June 28, 1996, C5.

————. "Paul V. McNutt Banquet Guest." February 25, 1938, X16.

————. "Philippine Pianist Gives Recital Tonight." September 7, 1924, 6.

————. "Ramon Magsaysay." March 18, 1957, A14.

————. "Society." October 20, 1921, 7.

————. "W. Morgan. Shuster, Publisher, Dies." May 27, 1960, B2.

————. "Wilson at Arlington." June 1, 1915, 1.

Washington Times. "Big Crowd Hears Philippine Band." March 5, 1909, 7.
———. "Capital Bows Head in Honor of Maine's Dead; Thousands See the Solemn Memorial Ceremony." March 23, 1912, 1.
———. "Eulogies Delivered on Philippine Hero." December 31, 1913, 4.
———. "GW Debaters to Meet Filipinos Over Islands." April 18, 1928, 5.

Archival Sources

Alexander Graham Bell Family Papers. Manuscript Division, Library of Congress.
Bernard M. Baruch Papers. Public Policy Papers, Department of Special Collections, Princeton University Library.
Diary of Basilio J. Valdes. The Philippine Diary Project.
Guillermo Tolentino, Edith Bolling Galt Wilson Papers, 1920–56. Manuscript Division, Library of Congress.
Lee, Brigadier General William L. Interview. Dwight D. Eisenhower Presidential Library and Museum, Abilene, Kansas, 1970.
Reverend Joseph A. Mulry, S.J. Collection. Georgetown University Library.

Index

ABOUT THE AUTHOR

Photo courtesy of Rasheed Hamdan.

    *E*rwin R. Tiongson is a professor at Georgetown University's Walsh School of Foreign Service. He teaches economics and writes about Philippine history. His essays have appeared in the Smithsonian's *Air and Space* magazine, the *New York Times*, *Positively Filipino*, *Slate*, the *Washington Post*, *Washingtonian* and the *White House History Quarterly*. He is co-founder of the Philippines on the Potomac (**POPDC**) Project.

Visit us at
www.historypress.com